Greening Spaces
for Worship and Ministry

Greening Spaces for Worship and Ministry

Congregations, Their Buildings, and Creation Care

MARK A. TORGERSON

 ALBAN

The Alban Institute
Herndon, Virginia

The Alban Institute
2121 Cooperative Way, Suite 100
Herndon, VA 20171

New Testament scripture quotations are from the New Revised Standard Version of the Bible, copyright © 1989, Division of Christian Education of the National Council of the Churches of Christ in the United States of America, and are used by permission.

Hebrew Bible (Old Testament) scripture quotations are reprinted from TANAKH: The Holy Scriptures: The New JPS Translation to the Tradi¬tional Hebrew Text, © 1988 by The Jewish Publication Society, with the permission of the publisher

Cover design by Signal Hill.

Library of Congress Cataloging-in-Publication Data
Torgerson, Mark Allen.
  Greening spaces for worship and ministry : congregations, their buildings, and creation care / Mark A. Torgerson.
      pages cm
  Includes bibliographical references and index.
  ISBN 978-1-56699-423-1
  1. Nature--Religious aspects--Christianity. 2. Human ecology-
-Religious aspects--Christianity. 3. Christian stewardship. 4. Church buildings--Design and construction. I. Title.
  BR115.N3T67 2012
  261.8'8--dc23
                                    2012010890

12   13   14   15   16   VG   5   4   3   2   1

Contents

Chapter 1
God, Humanity, and the Earth:
Interconnected and Interdependent
9

Blessing and Responsibility in Creation
Celebration of the Creator, Humanity, and the Earth
Covenant Wisdom
Consequences of Neglecting God's Commands
An Ideal of Shalom
Considering a Christian Witness
Pauline Reflections on the Creation
The End of All Things
Creation Care Responses to Scripture
Conclusions

125835

Energy Efficiency
Alternative Energy Systems and Cogeneration
Addressing the Building Shell

Chapter 7
The Interior Environments in Which We Live
161

Attention to Beauty
Indoor Air Quality
Product Selection
Green Walls, Living Walls, or Vertical Gardens
Occupant Comfort
Lighting Systems
Green Cleaning Programs
Final Thoughts on the Interior Environment

Chapter 8
Creation Care in Motion
185

Acknowledging the Need
Establishing a Commitment
Networking for Ideas and Support
Developing a Plan
Implementing the Plan
Education and Worship

Foreword

GOD'S EARTH IS SACRED AND FRAGILE. IN OUR DAY, WE ARE WITNESSING the rise in the Earth's population to seven billion people, with an ever greater demand for natural resources and energy. Before our eyes, the gradual shift in climate is beginning to impact farming, health, and the availability of fresh water supplies worldwide. Sometimes knowingly, sometimes unwittingly, we are posing the gravest of threats to the species of this Earth, including our own.

As leaders and members of faith communities, we are acutely aware of our sacred obligation to protect and support future generations. Our faith provides us with a spiritual mandate to seek justice and promote peace. The Genesis creation story, like that of many others, tells us explicitly that we are responsible as stewards of God's Earth. Many of us see that responsibility as a foundation of our faith. At the United Nations climate talks in Kyoto and Copenhagen, I served with diverse religious leaders of all the world's communities in voicing a common call to protect God's creation. How do we respond to this call, resonating with increasing urgency from our origin story to the present day? We have a powerful, readily available means of doing so: communities of faith represent the largest national and world constituency. We can build the political will to effect real, concrete change by building just and ecologically aware religious communities.

How fortunate to have an extraordinary new guide for all of our faith communities. Mark Torgerson's *Greening Spaces for Worship and Ministry: Congregations, Their Buildings, and*

Creation Care is a comprehensive guide for faith communities to respond to the critical challenges that our world is facing. Torgerson, a professor at Judson University, teaches in the area of theology, worship, and architecture.

With Torgerson as guide, we begin the conversation in our own faith communities, places of worship, and education, and seek to extend these conversations to the broader contemporary public sphere.

Professor Torgerson's encyclopedic work spans the critical dimensions of religion and the environment. He makes accessible the ancient texts and traditions found in Jewish and Christian faiths and the theological bases for developing an environmental ethic; explains the growth of diverse national religious polities that are responding to these issues; and puts into our hands a vast wealth of resources and guidance for religious communities.

Torgerson demonstrates his religious, environmental ethic through ten model faith communities around the country, each of which has taken a leadership role in framing ecologically aware, sacred architecture. Torgerson delves deeply into many of the most sophisticated and cutting-edge ecological issues for faith communities, including developing sustainable buildings, seeking beauty congruent with environmental principles, water management, green roofing, restoring adjacent prairie and wetlands, carpool parking, developing green teams, and integrating alternative energy fixtures, lighting, water systems, solar cells, and passive solar into one's community building. Meanwhile, Torgerson offers indispensable, concrete resources for religious communities at various stages of greening their congregations, from greening guides detailing possibilities for cost and implementation to suggestions for education and networking with other communities. Ultimately, he offers nothing short of a blueprint for religious environmental transformation.

I have worked with our Green Team at Temple Emanuel in our greater Washington, D.C., area for over twenty years and found Torgerson's guide both helpful—and hopeful. It is filled with innovative, creative approaches for furthering our ecological faith awareness, and for reaching out to our faith communities to effect real, meaningful change. It is thrilling to see the ways in which we can and must move forward over the next decade.

An ethics of creation care such as the one imagined by Torgerson will ultimately benefit not only humanity but all creation. Let us, guided and inspired by crucial conversations like these, walk more simply on this fragile Earth.

Rabbi Warren Stone
Co-chair, National Religion Coalition on Creation Care and
    Global Advisory Committee for Earth Day
Founding chair, Central Conference of American Rabbis
    Committee on the Environment
Rabbi, Temple Emanuel, Kensington, MD
climaterabbi.wordpress.com

Introduction

CREATION CARE IS A CONCERN THAT HAS CAPTURED THE ATTENTION OF our larger culture in recent decades. The world population has surpassed the seven billion mark, economic development around the world is increasing competition for natural resources, and remarkable amounts of waste are being produced around the planet. Whole species of plants and animals are disappearing with alarming regularity as more and more land is developed to address real and imagined needs. In spite of the increased pressure we are placing on the world, the beauty of the creation endures. The sun and moon provide light, rhythm, and energy. Rain falls, plants grow, and animals of all kinds seek to survive and even thrive. Scientists and photographic crews continue to reveal marvels of nature beyond our comprehension, teasing us with glimpses of interconnectedness that boggle the mind. In spite of cycles of human neglect of the environment, creation endures and continues to provide us with the necessities of life.

I am hopeful that as residents of this global community people of faith are warming to the idea of embracing God's instructions to serve and protect the creation (Gen. 2:15) with renewed vigor. In this book I would like to assist Jews and Christians in taking an active leadership role in both achieving creation care and modeling wise living to others. The buildings and property we use for worship and ministry represent a substantial visible presence in many communities. Our life choices affect our neighbors. Making green building strategies a high priority could physically represent our

1

belief that the creation is a gift from God entrusted to our care for the time being. We could help restore the natural world and lead our communities to treasure human and nonhuman life.

Our exploration of creation care will begin with the sacred scriptures of Judaism and Christianity. Select passages will be examined in chapter 1 in order to identify how God, humanity, and the nonhuman creation are to relate to one another. Hebrew Bible passages are drawn from the books of Genesis, Leviticus, Deuteronomy, Psalms, Isaiah, Hosea, and Jeremiah. New Testament passages featured are found in Romans, Ephesians, Colossians, 2 Peter, and Revelation. Theological concepts such as shalom, *bal tashchit*, and *tikkun olam* are also included. Chapter 1 concludes with a brief discussion of how Jewish and Christian understandings have sparked numerous organizations to promote and facilitate creation care. We have many resources to help us achieve our goals.

Chapter 2 addresses the cultivation of a creation care consciousness. Awareness of population growth and the accompanying pressures of natural resource consumption and waste production are noted. National initiatives promoting ecological stewardship and the recent rise in ecological awareness are mentioned to locate congregational efforts within a broader cultural agenda. Ecological footprint determination and life-cycle thinking are introduced as possible tools to consider the long-term impact that our life choices have on the world and its resources. A number of guides are identified for their wisdom and support for establishing a creation care plan for congregational life.

Chapter 3 examines green building as a tangible expression of creation care. The spectrum of levels at which green building could be pursued, including high performance, sustainability, restoration, and regeneration, are briefly mentioned. Congregations can pursue a variety of goals in the name of green building. The present state of green building is discussed to alert congregations to the support they can expect to find in the marketplace. Certification and labeling programs, the Energy Star program, the Interfaith Power and Light initiative, and Leadership in Energy and Environmental Design are discussed in detail. Each of these programs provides a congregation with substantial assistance in fulfilling green building goals. The special needs of historic buildings are raised here as well. Historic buildings often have features that naturally support creation care. Examples of historic projects that embrace creation care priorities and resources are included.

Chapter 4 introduces ten congregations from across North America that have pursued creation care in their green building activities. Keystone Community Church, Ada, Michigan; St. Gabriel of the Sorrowful Virgin Church, Toronto, Ontario; Congregation Beth David, San Luis Obispo, California; Jewish Reconstructionist Congregation, Evanston, Illinois; and Holy Wisdom Monastery, Middleton, Wisconsin, represent new construction projects. Temple Emanuel, Kensington, Maryland; Annunciation of the Mother of God Byzantine Catholic Church, Homer Glen, Illinois; and Pulaski Heights United Methodist Church, Little Rock, Arkansas, represent renovation or expansion projects. Museum at Eldridge Street and Eldridge Street Synagogue, New York, New York, and Unity Temple Unitarian Universalist Congregation, Oak Park, Illinois, represent historic preservation projects. The congregations are located in differing climatic regions and reflect a range of creation care initiatives. Their achievements in green building provide concrete examples to consider and provide tangible models for others.

Chapters 5, 6, and 7 contain a more detailed analysis of particular dimensions of green building that is illustrated by examples from the ten congregations noted in chapter 4. Chapter 5 addresses issues related to land development. Site selection, storm-water management, heat island effect, site lighting, and transportation to and from a site are addressed as primary topics. Chapter 6 examines the building shell. Architectural design, material selection, water consumption and wastewater disposal, and energy efficiency are discussed. Chapter 7 focuses on the development of the interior environment. Attention to beauty, indoor air quality, product selection, occupant comfort, lighting, and cleaning programs can be found here. Each of these three chapters contains explanations of concepts and options that will be invaluable for working through new construction, renovation, and historic preservation planning and design.

Chapter 8 concludes the book with reflections for developing and fulfilling creation care initiatives. Suggestions for helping congregations acknowledge global environmental pressures, embrace a biblical mandate for creation care, establish a commitment to green building, develop a plan, network, and implement the agreed-upon plan are included. The suggestions build on the large number of tools and resources identified throughout the book, providing an overall strategy for seeking to be faith-based agents mobilized to protect and serve the creation.

Two appendices and an annotated bibliography are found at the end of the book. Appendix A contains entries for creation care oriented website resources from many different religious movements within Judaism and Christianity. The appendix includes educational materials, worship materials, policy statements exhibiting the commitments of religious bodies, green building suggestions, and stories of individuals and congregations that are fulfilling creation care.

Appendix B provides a chart summarizing the green building features of the ten congregations noted in chapter 4. Within three categories—land development, building shell, and interior environment—details concerning the date of construction or renovation, size of the project, architectural firms involved, approximate costs, and LEED details are noted.

An annotated bibliography is also included. The bibliography has four sections: biblical and theological resources (for establishing a religious mandate to fulfill creation care), congregational articles and resources (materials featuring or developed by the ten congregations associated with this book), ecumenical and denominational resources for green building, and nonreligious green building resources. Brief annotations accompany most entries to guide the reader interested in exploring particular topics in more detail.

My hope is that this book will give confidence, language, inspiration, and understanding to congregations seeking to live faithfully in the midst of God's glorious world.

Acknowledgments

A project of this type cannot be accomplished by the efforts of a single individual. Although one person authored the book, a host of people actively shared in this effort. Sincere appreciation and thanks need to be extended to the congregations and individuals who freely invested in developing the content of this book:

Keystone Community Church, Ada, Michigan, especially the Reverend Gene DeJong, the Reverend Tom Emigh, and Luc VerMulm;

St. Gabriel of the Sorrowful Virgin Church, Toronto, Ontario, especially Father Paul Cusack and project architect Roberto Chiotti;

Congregation Beth David, San Luis Obispo, California, especially Rabbi Scott Corngold, Michael Blum, Paul Wolff, Linda Reitner, Sylvia Drucker, and project architect Ken Haggard;

Jewish Reconstructionist Congregation, Evanston, Illinois, especially Rabbi Brant Rosen, Sharon Diaz, Freddie Greenberg, Jill Persin, and architects Carol Ross Barney and Michael A. Ross;

Holy Wisdom Monastery, Middleton, Wisconsin, especially Sister Mary David Walgenbach, Sister Joanne Kollasch, Sister Lynn Smith, Neal Smith, Carolyn McGinley, and Scott Pigeon, associate with design and build firm Hoffman LLC;

Temple Emanuel, Kensington, Maryland, especially Rabbi Warren Stone and project architect Robert Schwartz;

Annunciation of the Mother of God Byzantine Catholic Church, Homer Glen, Illinois, especially Father Thomas J. Loya;

Pulaski Heights United Methodist Church, Little Rock, Arkansas, especially the Reverend Britt Skarda, Scharmel Roussel, and Jim Spradley;

Museum at Eldridge Street and Eldridge Street Synagogue, New York, New York, especially Director of the Museum at Eldridge Street Amy Stein Milford;

Unity Temple Unitarian Universalist Congregation, Oak Park, Illinois, especially the Reverend Alan Taylor, Barbara Moline, Mark Nussbaum, and Director of the Unity Temple Restoration Foundation Emily Roth;

Judson University, Elgin, Illinois, colleagues Laurie Braaten, Christopher Miller, and Robert Wallace, who contributed substantial comments to various portions of the manuscript; Paul Mouw, who shared manuscript production insight and technical support; Provost Dale Simmons and Dean Lanette Poteete-Young for support in writing and research; and the library staff for the cheerful and efficient acquisition of many books and articles;

Alban Institute staff and associates, including editorial assistance from Beth Ann Gaede and Andrea Lee, whose attention to detail and wise counsel helped to produce a more readable and coherent text; Kristy Pullen for the invitation to pursue this project; and Lauren Belen for artistic assistance in overall design.

Special thanks to my wife, Tracy, and children, Lukas and Elissa. Working on a project of this magnitude requires many months of focused effort that inevitably affects family life. Permission to invest the time and energy needed, occasional research assistance, and ongoing encouragement to complete this book have been much appreciated. And Tracy's modeling of the very creation care values and practices in our own household has inspired my own desire to share the importance of this life orientation.

While many voices have contributed to the development of this book, it is important to note that any and all errors remain my responsibility alone. It has been a pleasure and joy to develop this project. It is my sincere hope that faith communities of all kinds will find the content of this book to be a source of inspiration and action in pursuing green building as a part of a comprehensive effort to embody creation care on a daily basis.

CHAPTER 1

God, Humanity, and the Earth: Interconnected and Interdependent

The earth is the Lord's and all that it holds, the world and
its inhabitants.

Psalm 24:1

The Lord God took the man and placed him in the garden
of Eden, to till it and tend it.

Genesis 2:15

Scripture has been a source of instruction and inspiration for creation care for both Judaism and Christianity. Ecologically sensitive biblical and theological scholars have been reflecting upon the primary relationship between God, humanity, and the earth with renewed energy in the past forty years.[1] Certain themes of creation care and texts that support responsible behaviors toward the earth have emerged as a result of this scholarship and are frequently cited in published materials and denominational statements. A handful of these biblical passages from the Hebrew Bible and Christian

Scriptures will be examined in this chapter to establish a mandate for congregational green building initiatives.

BLESSING AND RESPONSIBILITY IN CREATION

Judaism has a rich collection of sacred writings collectively called the Tanakh. The Tanakh contains three types of writings, the Torah (the teachings or instruction), the Nevi'im (the prophets), and the Ketuvim (the writings).[2] The primary focus of the Tanakh is on living life as God intended in this world, and it says little about the afterlife. Occasionally, passages from these writings refer to the relationship between God, humanity, and the earth. For example, the first two chapters of the first book in the Torah, Genesis, contain reflections on the origin of the earth and everything it contains. God's role as creator of the earth and the whole cosmos is noted in two different creation accounts. In chapter 1, the author uses poetic language to describe the orderly way in which God initiates heaven and earth. Light, land, sea, vegetation, creatures of all kinds, and human beings are explicit movements within the creation drama. Punctuating these stages of the creation is the affirmation, "And God saw that this was good" (Gen. 1:10, 12, 18, 21, 25). God is the creative force behind the earth and its inhabitants. The world exists because of God's initiative and imagination. In a fundamental sense, the earth does not ultimately belong to humanity. God is the owner of the earth and its contents, and God delights in the creation.

The creation of humanity is first mentioned in Genesis 1:26–28. In three verses, the intimate connection between God and people, the blessing God has given humanity, and our responsibility to the earth are outlined:

> And God said, "Let us make man in our image, after our likeness. They shall rule the fish of the sea, the birds of the sky, the cattle, the whole earth, and all the creeping things that creep on earth." And God created man in His image, in the image of God

He created him; male and female He created them. God blessed them and God said to them, "Be fertile and increase, fill the earth and master it; and rule the fish of the sea, the birds of the sky, and all the living things that creep on earth."[3]

Humanity is created as male and female, material forms that serve to reflect the very image of God. A profound intimacy is implied in this relationship between God and people. Our connection to God's image sets us apart from the rest of the creation.[4] Interpreters understand that being created in the image of God bestows two unique gifts on humanity: knowledge of God and responsibility toward the earth. The command for people to master and rule the earth is articulated as a *blessing*. Exercising authority over the creation is not to be an autonomous or arbitrary expression of power but gracious acts performed by those who represent the interests of the Creator.[5] Genesis 1:31a articulates a final exclamation of delight in the creation, "And God saw all that He had made, and found it very good." The whole earth is found to be pleasing to God, and humanity is given a special blessing to treasure God's delight.

Genesis 2 presents a second narrative celebrating the creation of human beings and our relationship to God and the earth. In verse 7a we hear that the substance that constitutes humanity emerges from the earth: "The Lord God formed man ['*adam* in Hebrew] from the dust of the earth ['*adamah* in Hebrew]." The very language used to express this creative act links humanity to the earth in an intimate fashion. Humanity relies upon the earth as its ongoing source of life. In verse 7b we hear another expression of the close relationship between people and God: "He blew into his nostrils the breath of life, and man became a living being." Human life is initiated by nothing less than the breath of God. The special place of human beings in the created order is affirmed through this verse.

The primary charge of humanity's responsibility for the ground is found in Genesis 2:15: "The Lord God took the man and placed him in the garden of Eden, to till it and tend it." Biblical scholar Kristin Swenson indicates that the intended meaning of the words *till* (*'bd* in Hebrew) and *tend* (*šmr* in Hebrew) are "serve" and "protect."[6] Responsibility to care for the earth (inside and outside of the garden) is a service rendered to God, the source and owner of the land. As people care for the land in this reverential way, the land will care for the people in yielding its bounty. A mutual service is achieved and God is honored. In considering the roles Genesis 2 establishes between God, humanity, and the earth, theologian Jeremy Benstein offers an illustration in the form of a metaphor. God can be thought of as a king who wants to host many guests at a feast. Humanity represents the honored guests who are invited to enjoy a feast in the king's house, the earth. As guests we may use the resources of the king as we wish, but it would be disrespectful to destroy the house of the king.[7] Benstein's illustration accentuates the intrinsic order of creation, the interrelatedness between the Creator and the created, and the need to observe wise limits. Humanity is blessed with the opportunity to enjoy the bounty of the earth, but we are to do this as witnesses to the generosity and wisdom of the king.

CELEBRATION OF THE CREATOR, HUMANITY, AND THE EARTH

The book of Psalms celebrates in word and song the role of the Creator, the place of humanity, and the significance of the earth. Psalms contains one hundred and fifty hymns divided into five individual books, intended for worship celebrations. Many of these hymns celebrate the wonder and joy of both the Creator and the creation. Praise of the Creator is required of all that has been created.

The unique role of human beings in the created order is remembered and celebrated early in the Psalter collection. Psalm 8 is a composition of praise that accents the important responsibility entrusted to humanity. In Psalm 8:2, 4–10 we hear:

O Lord, our Lord, how majestic is Your name throughout the earth, You have covered the heavens with Your splendor! . . . When I behold Your heavens, the work of Your fingers, the moon and stars that You set in place, what is man that You have been mindful of him, mortal man that You have taken note of him, that You have made him little less than divine, and adorned him with glory and majesty; You have made him master over Your handiwork, laying the world at his feet, sheep and oxen, all of them, and wild beasts, too; the birds of the heavens, the fish of the sea, whatever travels the paths of the seas. O Lord, our Lord, how majestic is Your name throughout the earth!

The psalmist recognizes the close connection between God and people, but also acknowledges the distinction between the two. Remembering the authority and trust God grants humanity evokes joy. The unique authority that humanity is given over the creation is acclaimed. Here, authority is best interpreted as blessing to promote God's original intention, which is for the entire earth to proclaim God's glory forever.

Different dimensions of the relationship between God, the earth, and humanity are underscored as the reader encounters the Psalter. While human responsibility toward the earth is a primary focus in Psalm 8, God's ownership of the earth takes center stage in Psalm 24:1: "The earth is the Lord's and all that it holds, the world and its inhabitants." Recognition of this truth is a prerequisite for approaching the King of Glory. Biblical scholar Robert Wallace identifies a shift from an anthropocentric focus in Psalm 8 to an "ecocentric" focus in Psalm 104.[8] Psalm 104 is a hymn to the Creator celebrating many aspects of the creation of which humanity is simply one part: light, clouds, winds, fire, water, mountains, valleys, mammals, birds, grass, trees, sun, moon, and earth itself. The first twenty verses remember God's initiation of the heavens and earth. Verse 24 accents the praise of God for much creative work: "How many are the things You have made, O Lord; You have made them all with wisdom; the earth is full of Your creation." God's role as creator and sovereign owner is celebrated in these psalms.

Psalm 148 accents an ecocentric focus as well. Verses 3–10 direct God's entire creation to praise the author of all that exists:

Praise Him, sun and moon, praise Him, all bright stars.
Praise Him, highest heavens, and you waters that are above the heavens.
Let them praise the name of the Lord, for it was He who commanded that they be created. He made them endure forever, establishing an order that shall never change.
Praise the Lord, O you who are on earth, all sea monsters and ocean depths, fire and hail, snow and smoke, storm wind that executes His command, all mountains and hills, all fruit trees and cedars, all wild and tamed beasts, creeping things and winged birds.

The command for all dimensions of the created order to praise God undermines the idea that the earth exists merely to be raw material available for human consumption. This song recognizes God's continuing role as creator and sovereign king over all the cosmos. The earth, in all of its material expressions, exists primarily for the glory of God. These psalms challenge humanity to see itself as one part of a vast created order, *all of which* is intended to praise the Lord.

COVENANT WISDOM

In addition to the command to praise God, Scripture provides instructions that enable people to adequately navigate their responsibilities toward God, the earth, and one another. The Torah is a gift of theological insight with implications for the concrete ways in which we fulfill our responsibilities. The books of Leviticus and Deuteronomy contain many teachings pertaining to covenant life that correlate with creation care. In covenant living, time itself is divided into cycles of work and rest. Human beings and the earth are subject to times of labor and restoration. Sabbath days, sabbath years, and the year of jubilee are examples of the restorative cycle God has in mind for humanity and the earth.[9]

Deuteronomy 5:13–14 states: "Six days you shall labor and do all your work, but the seventh day is a sabbath of the Lord your

God; you shall not do any work." God provides the model for this cycle of rest in Genesis 1 when after the sixth day of creation he rests. Humanity is to observe the same cycle of rest to honor the God who initiated all things. Benefits from this rest include restored energy and a prescribed length of time to linger in the blessings of the earth. In commenting on the ideal of sabbath, David Ehrenfeld and Philip J. Bentley note:

> On the Sabbath, the traditionally observant Jew does more than rest, pray, and refrain from ordinary work. There are at least three other elements of Sabbath observance which are relevant to stewardship: we create nothing, we destroy nothing, and we enjoy the bounty of the earth. In this way, the Sabbath becomes a celebration of our tenancy and stewardship in the world.[10]

Observing sabbath reminds us of our relationship to God, that God is creator and we are created. We remember that God is sovereign, sustainer of all, and ultimate owner independent of human effort. At times our sabbath observance means that we refrain from using the material of this world, a reminder that it does not exist solely for our consumption. Thus, our appreciation of the earth's bounty is heightened. God, humanity, and the earth benefit from a regular weekly cycle of rest and reflection.

With this weekly sabbath rhythm, the land itself receives a respite from cultivation and development one day out of seven, but experiences a more dramatic benefit from the sabbath of years and ultimate year of jubilee. Leviticus 25 commands a seven-year cycle of land use and rest: the land is cultivated for six years and during the seventh year complete rest is observed. When seven cycles of seven years have passed, forty-nine years in all, the fiftieth year is to be a year of restoration—a jubilee. Land redistribution is also to be achieved in this fiftieth year in order to restore the economic potential of those who have become marginalized through the years. Appreciation of the Creator who bestowed the land as a gift is inherent in these observances. Humanity is reminded that we have temporary use of the land, but that God is the ultimate owner of all things. The year of jubilee provides an opportunity to renew our relationship with the Creator, with our neighbor, and with the land we occupy.

The ideals behind the covenant commands of sabbath and jubilee may seem unattainable in a culture characterized by unbridled consumption, maximum production, and personal exhaustion. The commodification of time itself creates pressure to constantly plan and work. In this cultural mindset, it is all too easy to view natural resources as only raw materials waiting to be pressed into service. The idea of sabbath challenges such a consumption-without-renewal orientation. God's wisdom and command for humanity and the earth is to refrain from an endless cycle of work and consumption. When we honor sabbath cycles, opportunities for praising God as the source of all life, experiencing refreshment from human labor, and encouraging renewal of the earth emerge. It is clear from these commands that God has expectations for our stewardship of the earth. God's people are called to be countercultural in their treatment of one another and the creation.

A significant ecological principle in Judaism today, *bal tashchit*, is rooted in a rabbinic interpretation of Deuteronomy 20:19–20 (Rambam, *Hilkhot Melakhim* 6:10). *Bal tashchit* is based upon a specific prohibition against unnecessary destruction (acts that inhibit the sustaining of life) and embraces a more comprehensive understanding of stewardship. Addressing the devastation of nature caused by war, the Deuteronomy passage identified a limit that was imposed on an army, even in the heat of battle:

> When in your war against a city you have to besiege it a long time in order to capture it, you must not destroy its trees, wielding the ax against them. You may eat of them, but you must not cut them down. Are trees of the field human to withdraw before you into the besieged city? Only trees that you know do not yield food may be destroyed; you may cut them down for constructing siegeworks against the city that is waging war on you, until it has been reduced.

The phrase "must not destroy" inspired *bal tashchit*. Unnecessary damage to the environment, even in the midst of battle, is forbidden. Rabbinic scholars have interpreted this passage to be a prohibition against a wide range of acts of destruction toward the natural world, including cutting off water to trees, overgrazing, unjustifiably killing animals, destroying cultivated plant variet-ies, polluting air and water, overconsuming anything, and wasting mineral resources.[11] Nineteenth-century rabbi Samson Raphael Hirsch has summed up the intention of *bal tashchit*:

> "Do not destroy anything!" is the first and most general call of God, which comes to you, man, when you realize yourself as master of the earth. . . . God's call proclaims to you . . . , "If you destroy, if you ruin—at that moment you are not a man, you are an animal, and have no right to the things around you. I lent them to you for wise use only; never forget that I lent them to you. As soon as you use them unwisely, be it the greatest or the smallest, you commit treachery against My world, you commit murder and robbery against My property, you sin against Me!"[12]

Hirsch's understanding and application of *bal tashchit* emphasizes the relationships that exist between God, humanity, and the earth. God entrusts humanity to work in the world and to use the gifts of this world wisely. We are not given permission to abuse the limits of our authority. To fulfill the steward's role God has granted us, we must respect God, other people, and the world around us. Hirsch's understanding of *bal tashchit* challenges people of faith to *bear witness to God's original intentions* for humanity and the natural world. In following *bal tashchit*, we can honor the God whose world we occupy, implement our creation care authority (to serve and protect) with grace, and allow the natural world to praise its Creator through its beauty and wonder.

CONSEQUENCES OF NEGLECTING GOD'S COMMANDS

The intimacy between humanity and the dust of the earth is un-derscored by biblical descriptions of the consequences that occur when people choose not to obey God. Violating God's commands yields negative consequences for the land. The first evidence of the land suffering at the hands of humanity is found in Genesis 3. This story recalls Adam and Eve's choice to disobey God by eating from the tree of knowledge of good and bad—the only tree in the Garden of Eden whose fruit they were forbidden to eat. The intimate connection between humanity and the earth is remembered in Genesis 3:17–19 as God pronounces punishment that affects the land:

> To Adam He said, "Because you did as your wife said and ate of
>   the tree about which I commanded you, 'You shall not eat
>   of it,'
> Cursed be the ground because of you;
> By toil shall you eat of it
> All the days of your life:
> Thorns and thistles shall it sprout for you.
> But your food shall be the grasses of the field;
> By the sweat of your brow
> Shall you get bread to eat,
> Until you return to the ground—
> For from it you were taken.
> For dust you are,
> And to dust you shall return."

Our responses to God's commands affect the very earth upon which we depend. The earth suffers when we choose not to follow God's directions for living. An important reality is acknowledged here. When considering environmental stewardship today, neglecting God's wisdom for creation care yields primary suffering for the earth and hardships for humanity, who remains dependent on it.

Deuteronomy records consequences for the land that occur when the people abandon their commitment to God's covenant. Calamity results from such choices and spills over into the land the people occupy. Deuteronomy 11:13–17 recalls that when people fail to fulfill God's expectations for covenant living drought and famine will follow. Idolatry is a primary concern in the text. In our day, idolatry can take many forms. While many of us may not literally bow down and worship an object we assign divine status, we do often elevate our own interests to a central place in our lives and make life choices that may have destructive consequences (intentional or unintentional) for our relationships to God, other people, and the natural world. Scientific studies conducted in the last twenty years have confirmed a direct relationship between human activities and degradation of our earth. Acid rain, desertification, rapid species extinction, and an increase in the levels of carbon dioxide in the atmosphere are examples of negative effects our choices are having on God's world. Ignoring covenant wisdom contributes to the destruction of the land.

The writings of the prophets of Scripture also reveal the intimate link between humanity and the earth. The prophet Isaiah, thought to have lived in the eighth century BCE, challenged the Southern Kingdom of Judah to fulfill covenant living or be subject to the threat of Assyrian invasion. Isaiah 24:4–6 describes the withering and languishing of the earth that follows breaking covenant:

> The earth is withered, sear; the world languishes, it is sear; the most exalted people of the earth languish. For the earth was defiled under its inhabitants; because they transgressed teachings, violated laws, broke the ancient covenant. That is why a curse consumes the earth, and its inhabitants pay the penalty; that is why earth's dwellers have dwindled, and but few men are left.

The people's choice not to live in conformity with the laws of the covenant bore consequences for the earth. The prophet's words hearken back to Genesis 3, where the earth suffers because of humanity's choice to violate its relationship with God. The future of humanity and the earth remain intrinsically linked. Conformity to the instructions of God yields life for people and the earth; violation of the teachings yields destruction for both.

Hosea's oracles came to the people of the Northern Kingdom just prior to the kingdom's destruction by the Assyrian Empire in the eighth century BCE. All life on the earth suffers as a consequence of the people God's failure to uphold their promises. In Hosea 4:1–3 the prophet proclaims:

Hear the word of the Lord, O people of Israel!
For the Lord has a case
Against the inhabitants of this land,
Because there is no honesty and no goodness
And no obedience to God in the land.
[False] swearing, dishonesty, and murder,
And theft and adultery are rife;
Crime follows upon crime!
For that, the earth is withered;
Everything that dwells on it languishes—
Beasts of the field and birds of the sky—
Even the fish of the sea perish.

God has been gracious in providing instructions for how to care for and enjoy all of the creation. God's people are to be the model stewards who show others how best to honor the Creator and the creation he has entrusted to us. If God's people continue to abandon their primary responsibilities for fulfilling covenant life, then the very existence of all creation is in jeopardy.

Jeremiah, a prophet of the late seventh and early sixth centuries BCE, followed Isaiah in challenging the people of Judah to recommit themselves to covenant living. Jeremiah 12:10–13 identifies the degradation of the land as a consequence of the people of God's failure to live according to the covenant:

Many shepherds have destroyed My vineyard,
Have trampled My field,
Have made My delightful field
A desolate wilderness.
They have made her a desolation;
Desolate; she pours out grief to Me.
The whole land is laid desolate.
But no man give it thought.
Spoilers have come:
Upon all the bare heights of the wilderness.
For a sword of the Lord devours
From one end of the land to the other;
No flesh is safe.
They have sown wheat and reaped thorns,
They have endured pain to no avail.
Be shamed, then, by your harvest—
By the blazing wrath of the Lord!

The earth suffers at the hands of the people who are to treasure it, and the creation cries out to God. God allows the people to live with the consequences of their disobedience. The earth and humanity suffer together again as they did in Genesis 3. Often in Scripture God's punishment is a natural consequence of breaking covenant. We would not be amiss to interpret our struggles with environmental degradation as a consequence of our continuing neglect to fulfill God's instructions to serve and protect the creation.

The biblical prophets also speak of hope for the earth. As noted above, Hosea identified the people's failures, but he also proclaimed God's promise of restoration. Hosea 2:20–25 foresees a renewal of covenant yielding renewed life for the earth:

> In that day, I will make a covenant for them with the beasts of
>   the field, the birds of the air, and the creeping things of the
>   ground; I will also banish bow, sword, and war from the
>   land. Thus I will let them lie down in safety.
> And I will espouse you forever:
> I will espouse you with righteousness and justice,
> And with goodness and mercy,
> And I will espouse you with faithfulness;
> Then you shall be devoted to the Lord.
> In that day,
> I will respond
> —declares the Lord—
> I will respond to the sky,
> And it shall respond to the earth;
> And the earth shall respond
> With new grain and wine and oil,
> And they shall respond to Jezreel.
> I will sow her in the land as My own;
> And take Lo-ruhamah back in favor;
> And I will say to Lo-amni, "You are My people,"
> And he will respond, "[You are] my God."

This passage highlights the positive impact on animal life, ground, and sky that will be achieved through renewal of covenant life. God's vision for humanity and the earth is that they will live together in harmony. The writings of Hosea remind us that covenant living involves an existence inclusive of the earth.

Although this is only a brief sampling of prophetic proclamations concerning the intimate relationship between God's people and the earth, it demonstrates the way God has ordered the world. Fulfilling covenant life is not merely a matter of personal preference or of consequence only for God's people. The messages of God's prophets illustrate the interdependent nature of life in this world. Embodying covenant will yield the fullness of God's intentions for all life—human and nonhuman—in God's world.

AN IDEAL OF *SHALOM*

A holistic vision of life can be found in the Hebrew Bible, a vision that perhaps is best summarized in the word *shalom*. Shalom is a Hebrew word that means safety, fulfillment, peace, harmony, and completeness. Within Judaism, shalom functions as a greeting when people meet and as a word of blessing when they part. In passages such as Isaiah 2:1–4, Isaiah 11:1–9, and Ezekiel 47:1–12, shalom is a goal for humanity to pursue, a goal to keep in mind when pursuing creation care. Although the passages do not always explicitly use the word *shalom*, restoring the creation is in fact the pursuit of shalom. Isaiah 11:6–9 anticipates restoration in this way:

> The wolf shall dwell with the lamb,
> The leopard lie down with the kid;
> The calf, the beast of prey, and the fatling together,
> With a little boy to herd them.
> The cow and the bear shall graze,
> Their young shall lie down together;
> And the lion, like the ox, shall eat straw.
> A babe shall play
> Over a viper's hole,
> And an infant pass his hand
> Over an adder's den.
> In all of My sacred mount
> Nothing evil or vile shall be done;
> For the land shall be filled with devotion to the Lord
> As water covers the sea.

Isaiah's vision here is of a world restored according to God's original intentions for the human and nonhuman creation. Achieving this ultimate vision entails our pursuit of relationships with God, one another, and the earth according to covenant living. Our participation in creation care is a part of seeking to embody this shalom ideal. How are we working toward this goal? Are we doing everything within our power to promote the interdependence of all created life, or are we hindering God's desires for creation? In each of the texts anticipating shalom, the prophets expect that life in this world will be restored according to God's original intentions for people and the larger creation. Intimately connected to God's restoration is our obedience to God's commandments for covenant living. Right relationships between God and God's people and between God's people and the earth are intertwined. This guiding vision of justice, harmony, and wholeness challenges and inspires us in our contemporary creation care efforts.

CONSIDERING A CHRISTIAN WITNESS

Christians also affirm the inspired revelation of God's word as recorded in the Hebrew Bible. Creation care statements that refer to Hebrew Bible (Old Testament) texts frequently cite the Genesis and Psalms passages noted above. The theological affirmations discussed—including God as the initiator and source of creation, humanity as entrusted with stewardship responsibilities toward the earth, the presence of brokenness due to disobedience, the necessity of covenant living, and a future restoration for creation—are shared by Christians. The Christian tradition also recognizes the need to pursue right relationships between God, humanity, and the earth, and the Christian canon builds upon this divine revelation. Central to a Christian understanding of God at work in the world is the person of Jesus Christ. According to Christian biblical interpreters and theologians seeking to promote creation care, the life, death, and resurrection of Jesus Christ facilitates the ultimate fulfillment of shalom for the whole created order.

Debate has arisen in Christian circles over whether creation will ultimately be destroyed or renewed. The differing views seem to align with one of two understandings: whether one believes that the redemptive work of God in Christ applies only to humanity or to the entire created order. Those who believe that the redemption made possible by Jesus Christ applies only to people generally think of the created world as human centered. In this human-centered vision of creation, the material world is disposable and of value only in relation to human use. Ultimately, the destruction of the natural world is of no eternal consequence for humanity, and thus of no consequence to God. Those who believe that the redemption of Jesus Christ applies to both humanity and the nonhuman created world generally envision creation as God centered. They believe the material world is of great value for its own sake as well as in relation to human beings. A God-centered view takes seriously the goodness of the material world as expressed in Genesis, that God treasures *both* the nonhuman creation and humanity. The apostle Paul's reflections on the restoration of all things in heaven and earth in Christ are consistent with a God-centered vision. Both humanity and the nonhuman creation are in need of redemption (consistent with earlier observations from Genesis 3), and both will be restored at the end of all things. Nonhuman creation is important to God both in the here and now and in future life to come.

PAULINE REFLECTIONS ON THE CREATION

The apostle Paul, the first century CE Christian missionary, affirmed God as creator of the cosmos who is sovereign over all things. Paul also acknowledged the presence of sin in the world because of humanity's initial disobedience through Adam and the need for humanity's relationship with God to be restored. In his letter to the churches in Rome, Paul mentions the effects of sin upon the whole created order and recognizes the implications of Christ's redeeming actions for the entire creation. In Romans 8:19–23 Paul writes:

> For the creation waits with eager longing for the revealing of the children of God; for the creation was subjected to futility, not of its own will but by the will of the one who subjected it, in hope that the creation itself will be set free from its bondage to decay and will obtain the freedom of the glory of the children of God. We know that the whole creation has been groaning in labor pains until now; and not only the creation, but we ourselves, who have the first fruits of the Spirit, groan inwardly while we wait for adoption, the redemption of our bodies.

For Paul, redemption includes the material cosmos. He recognizes that the creation that was called to praise the Creator has been hindered by the presence of sin in the world. Creation as well as humanity have been damaged by sin (a reference to the intimate connection established in Genesis). Sin's redemption, initiated by Christ's death and resurrection, has not yet come to fruition. The fullness of redemption involves the whole created order—human and nonhuman—including the restoration of the material world.

References to the cosmic impact of Christ on the creation can be found in letters attributed to Paul that were written to Christian communities in Ephesus and Colossae (cities in Asia Minor). In these letters, redemption encompasses more than humanity. In Ephesians 1:8b–10 the author writes, "With all wisdom and insight he has made known to us the mystery of his will, according to his good pleasure that he set forth in Christ, as a plan for the fullness of time, to gather up all things in him, things in heaven and things on earth." Christ is portrayed as the ultimate redeemer of all creation. Everything—on earth and in heaven—will be restored in the fullness of time. The redemptive work of Christ has significance for all of the created order, not only for people.

The Pauline letter to the Christians in Colossae focuses on the cosmic dimensions of the work of Christ, but adds the initial creation to ultimate restoration. A striking example of this emphasis is found in Colossians 1:15–20:

He [Christ] is the image of the invisible God, the firstborn of all creation; for in him all things in heaven and on earth were created, things visible and invisible, whether thrones or dominions or rulers or powers—all things have been created through him and for him. He himself is before all things, and in him all things hold together. He is the head of the body, the church; he is the beginning, the firstborn from the dead, so that he might come to have first place in everything. For in him all the fullness of God was pleased to dwell, and through him God was pleased to reconcile to himself all things, whether on earth or in heaven, by making peace through the blood of his cross.

An ultimate theological claim for the person and work of Christ is found in this passage, identifying him as both creator and redeemer of all creation. The whole creation experiences relationship to Christ, and all things will be reconciled and restored through his sacrifice on the cross.

The content of Romans, Ephesians, and Colossians build on Hebrew Bible references to God as the sovereign creator of the cosmos. Through humanity's disobedience, sin has indeed permeated the entire creation, human and nonhuman. God has overcome the full effects of sin in the person and work of Jesus Christ. Redemption of the whole cosmos is a process that has begun, but has not yet to come to completion. Although some Christians conclude that Paul's understanding of redemption applies only to people, it is important to recognize that the writings cited here illustrate that his vision includes both human and nonhuman creation. Paul describes the church as "the body of Christ" and calls it to embody redemptive activities in the world. In light of Paul's teaching, creation care for Christians becomes not merely a good work to do on behalf of God and others but participation in the very redemptive activity of Christ.

THE END OF ALL THINGS

Christians interpret passages from the letter of 2 Peter and the book of Revelation to John (or Apocalypse) differently depending on whether the reader holds a human-centered or God-centered vision of the creation. Second Peter is a short letter written in the name of the apostle Peter sometime in the late first or early second century CE. Second Peter 3:10 describes the future of the creation: "But the day of the Lord will come like a thief, and then the heavens will pass away with a loud noise, and the elements will be dissolved with fire, and the earth and everything that is done on it will be disclosed." If a reader holds a human-centered vision of the creation, it is fairly easy to interpret this verse, and those that follow (vv. 11–13), as an indicator that this world will simply be annihilated. If annihilation is the future of the earth, then creation care itself will be necessary only until the moment of utter destruction (the original command to serve and protect remains potent only as long as *humanity* continues to inhabit the earth). The difficulty with the annihilation interpretation is that it does not seem to be consistent with either a Hebrew Bible, God-centered vision of the creation or Paul's understanding of the cosmic redemption to come in Christ. And if annihilation is the only future for this earth, it would imply that even God could not ultimately redeem the sin or brokenness that has distorted the whole creation.

However, annihilation of the creation is not the only way to read 2 Peter 3:10. The word *fire* is used in two ways in Christian Scriptures: both as a means of destruction and as a means of refinement (as in the refining process used in metallurgy). If a reader holds to a God-centered vision of creation it is possible to interpret 2 Peter 3:10 as referring to a coming refinement process. The writer foresees a coming examination of both heaven and earth. At the end of verse 10 the word *disclosed* appears. The disclosure to come will reveal all that needs to be purged. The purpose of the refinement process will be to purge all that is not consistent with God's original intentions for heaven and earth.[13] All things in heaven and on earth will be examined, purged, and renewed by God. Interpreting the intention of 2 Peter 3:10 in this way allows us to understand our creation care as participation in the renewal to come.

The Revelation to John, or the book of Revelation, contains visions of things that will come to pass at the end of the world. Mention is made in Revelation 11:18 of punishment for those who destroy the earth: "The nations raged, but your wrath has come, and the time for judging the dead, for rewarding your servants, the prophets and saints and all who fear your name, both small and great, and for destroying those who destroy the earth." The earth appears to remain valuable to God, as it was in the beginning, and those who destroy it are subject to punishment for their neglect. Throughout the book Christ's redemptive work takes place on a cosmic scale. The book ends with a final vision of the restoration of all things (Rev. 21:1–5):

> Then I saw a new heaven and a new earth; for the first heaven and the first earth had passed away, and the sea was no more. And I saw the holy city, the new Jerusalem, coming down out of heaven from God, prepared as a bride adorned for her husband. And I heard a loud voice from the throne saying,
> "See, the home of God is among mortals.
> He will dwell with them;
> they will be his peoples,
> and God himself will be with them;
> he will wipe every tear from their eyes.
> Death will be no more;
> mourning and crying and pain will be no more,
> for the first things have passed away."
> And the one who was seated on the throne said, "See, I am making all things new." Also he said, "Write this, for these words are trustworthy and true."

The phrases "for the first things have passed away" and "See, I am making all things new" in this text have been interpreted in two different ways by Christians: (1) that the old will be destroyed and a replacement will be created (the new); (2) that the old will be renewed or restored and thus become new. The first interpretation anticipates the destruction of the creation; the second, its restoration. The first interpretation is often held by those who hold a human-centered vision of creation; the second by those who hold a God-centered vision. In light of all that has been said thus far in this chapter about the value that God places on the creation and its expected restoration in and through Christ, the second understanding makes more sense. In reflecting on verse 5 in his commentary on Revelation, biblical scholar Eugene Boring observes: "God does not make 'all new things,' but 'all things new.'"[14] The new heaven and new earth that are to emerge in the wake of the redemptive work of Christ will be in continuity with our existing heaven and earth. A real transformation of the material world will occur in light of final judgment. Obliteration of the created world is not God's intention for creation. Rather, God would have God's people work in every redemptive way possible to participate even now in the ultimate transformation of all things.

CREATION CARE RESPONSES TO SCRIPTURE

An important Jewish environmental concept has emerged in concert with the biblical emphases noted above. *Tikkun olam* is a Hebrew phrase that means "world repair" or "repair of the world." *Tikkun olam* first appeared in the writings of the Mishnah (a postbiblical collection of oral traditions about the law, codified and recorded in the early third century CE) in relation to providing for those who may be at a disadvantage. In the sixteenth century the phrase took on an additional meaning through the writings of Jewish mystic Rabbi Isaac Luria. Rabbi Luria thought of acts of *tikkun olam* as ways of cooperating with God to restore wholeness to the world. Since the 1950s *tikkun olam* has been thought of as foundational for pursuing of social action of many kinds, including creation care. An active role in environmental restoration is an avenue to live out the command to serve and protect the creation. Today, many Jewish communities refer to their green synagogue efforts as an expression of *tikkun olam*.

Environmental organizations for education and political action emerged within Judaism from scholarly reflection on biblical wisdom and growing cultural concerns for environmental care. Only a handful of examples can be mentioned in this brief overview. The Shalom Center (www.theshalomcenter.org) was founded in 1983 by Rabbi Arthur Waskow as a division of the Reconstructionist Rabbinical College. Waskow, active in teaching, writing, and public reconciliation initiatives, established the Shalom Center, in part, to promote political engagement with multiple environmental issues. He has been working in the area of environmental care and faith since the late 1970s. He has written and edited significant works promoting creation care rooted in faith. The Shalom Center is now an independent, not-for-profit agency. The center provides resources for the pursuit of peace, justice, and earth healing within Judaism and between religious communities. Numerous print and multimedia resources for actively exploring creation care may be found via the center and its affiliates.

In 1988 *Shomrei Adamah*, "Keepers (Guardians) of the Earth," was founded by writer, teacher, and environmental advocate, Ellen Bernstein. Bernstein has authored and edited numerous books that promote congregational engagement in creation care. Shomrei Adamah was a movement that generated chapters in numerous locations. Shomrei Adamah of Greater Washington (DC) has been a particularly active chapter, founded on Earth Day in 1990 by Mike Tabor and De Herman. Shomrei Adamah of Greater Washington has remained active in local and national efforts to promote environmental education. News, programs, and connections to resources can be found through their website. A guide for greening synagogues has been produced and distributed with their assistance as well. Shomrei Adamah has been an effective catalyst for raising environmental awareness in synagogues and Jewish classrooms through publications, workshops, conferences, and outdoor activities.

In 1994 the Teva Learning Center (www.tevalearningcenter.org), a project initiated by the United Jewish Appeal (UJA) Federation of New York, began to develop a residential environmental education program for Jewish day-school students. The center, now Teva Learning Alliance, promotes creation care in concert with Jewish faith understandings (Conservative, Orthodox, and Reform). A thematic progression from awareness to interconnectedness to responsibility is at the heart of their programs for young people and adults. Opportunities for learning are extended through day school, congregational, community group, and wilderness experiences.

The development of an environmental consciousness within Judaism led to interfaith work. A 1992 gathering of leaders from Jewish and Christian communities led to the establishment of the National Religious Partnership for the Environment. The Coalition on the Environment and Jewish Life (COEJL; www.coejl. org) grew from this partnership initiative in 1993. The COEJL has worked across the spectrum of Jewish communities to build consensus on environmental issues, develop position statements, and participate in advocacy coalitions.[15] COEJL is a primary clearinghouse for creation care materials developed for Jewish congregations (Conservative, Orthodox, Reconstructionist, and Reform). COEJL is also one of four major organizations that constitute the National Religious Partnership for the Environment (www.nrpe. org), an interfaith coalition of Jewish and Christian movements. A link on the COEJL website, "Greening Synagogue Resources" connects people to materials relevant to buildings, grounds, purchasing equipment and supplies, programs for the congregation, education for youth and adults, and rabbinic insights for clergy.

Creation care has become a priority for Jewish communities across the country. Six additional websites for resources can be found in Appendix A. The mandate to be responsible stewards of the creation has been recognized and is being pursued in multiple ways. Creation care is being promoted in congregational life across the country in Shabbat services, in Passover celebrations, and through observances of *Tu B'Shvat* (the Jewish New Year of the Trees).[16] Educational activities of many kinds are helping the faithful of all ages to understand the necessity of creation care and to discover tangible ways to live responsibly. Local, state, and national initiatives are seeking to promote and support legislation that embraces environmental stewardship.

In the 1970s Christian communities began to acknowledge that people in Western Europe and North America had done little in the wake of the Industrial Revolution to recognize or address environmental exploitation. Theologians began challenging this passive posture on scriptural grounds. They began to identify environmental neglect as sin. They called for the church to confess its transgressions against the earth and for people to change their destructive lifestyle choices. Sporadic calls for change in the 1970s and 1980s evolved into more comprehensive attention to creation care beginning in the 1990s. A host of denominations within the Christian church promote responsible stewardship of the creation today via denominational statements and resolutions, curriculum, political and social action initiatives, national and regional conferences and workshops, local congregational programs, and networking with others (within and outside of denominational lines). A few examples of cooperative efforts are noted here.

The Evangelical Environmental Network (www.creationcare.org) has issued "On the Care of Creation: An Evangelical Declaration on the Care of Creation" (1993), publishes *Creation Care* magazine, and shares many resources addressing Scripture, education, and concrete actions of stewardship. The network resulted from collaboration between World Vision and Evangelicals for Social Action. It was established in 1993 to resource evangelical congregations. Approximately five hundred leaders of churches and institutions have formally endorsed this declaration and affiliated themselves with this network.

The National Council of Churches of Christ (www.nccecojustice.org) has established Eco-Justice Programs (networks, resources, initiatives, and stories for promoting environmental stewardship) for its member denominations. "God's Earth Is Sacred: An Open Letter to Church and Society in the United States" (2005) and a study guide for applying the content of this statement on the environment are examples of materials included on this website. Multiple documents for promoting creation care through church buildings can be found here as well. The National Council of Churches of Christ (NCC) is a coalition of thirty-four denominations (Protestant, Eastern Orthodox, and African American) that seek to promote understanding and cooperation among Christian denominations.

The National Religious Partnership for the Environment (NRPE; www.nrpe.org), established in 1993, has assembled a host of materials for understanding and pursuing environmental care.

The NRPE consists of four primary networks of Christians and Jews: the Coalition on the Environment and Jewish Life, the US Conference of Catholic Bishops, the National Council of Churches of Christ, and the Evangelical Environmental Network. This cooperative venture exemplifies the common vision among Jews and Christians for environmental stewardship.

Three other initiatives are noteworthy. First, Green Faith (www.greenfaith.org) is an interfaith organization supporting environmental leadership in congregations. Green Faith began in 1992 as Partners for Environmental Quality, founded by Jewish and Christian leaders in New Jersey. Energy conservation and promoting green energy use have been a primary focus of the organization. Additional dimensions of creation care were added in the early 2000s. A certification program is now available for congregations that would appreciate specific guidance and mentoring in achieving creation care. Second, Earth Ministry (www.earthministry.org) is a Christian initiative established in 1992 by area churches in Puget Sound, Washington. Earth Ministry has produced resources for education and worship,[17] sponsored workshops and conferences, developed courses with universities, and promoted legislation for promoting creation care. They actively collaborate on projects with a wide range of faith partners. They have also initiated a "Greening Congregations Program" for communities seeking assistance in fulfilling creation care. Third, Web of Creation (www.webofcreation.org) is a website maintained by the Lutheran School of Theology at Chicago. It is supported through a variety of faith-based agencies including the Eco-Justice Working Group of the National Council of Churches, Theological Education to Meet the Environmental Challenge, the Evangelical Lutheran Church in America, the Presbyterian Church (USA), and several Protestant seminaries. Resources related to education, worship, and greening initiatives of many kinds are available through the site.

Creation care has become a priority for many Christian communities. A whole array of denominational websites feature creation care oriented materials. Sixteen denominational websites are noted in appendix A. In developing creation care strategies, much can be learned from visiting a variety of denominational websites to read and review the posted position statements, theological understandings, curriculum, worship resources, stories of success, and initiatives in process. Learning from others will have a collateral benefit of encouraging mutual respect between traditions and will identify common ground for working with people of faith from multiple congregations.

CONCLUSIONS

When the fullness of the witness of the Hebrew Bible and Christian Scriptures are considered, a God-centered vision of the creation emerges. God is the creator of and sovereign over everything. All that God has created is good. Human and nonhuman life forms exist in intimate relationship to one another. Both occupy important roles in the overall plan for the creation. Humanity is given unique responsibilities to care for the nonhuman creation. Sin has permeated and distorted the entire creation, and all things are in need of redemption. Humanity is charged with working in ways that seek to restore the creation. For Christians, the death and resurrection of Jesus Christ provides the way through which all will be made new or whole. Scripture provides both a justification and a mandate for communities of faith to engage in creation care. Participating actively in creation care allows us to both fulfill our calling to be faithful stewards of all that has been entrusted to us and bear witness to the generosity and love of the Creator in whose image we are made.

The many organizations, networks, and initiatives established by Jewish and Christian communities, independently and together, demonstrate a continuing commitment to acting on the biblical mandate for creation care. A strong foundation has been established for a range of environmental activities, including green building, which is the focus of this book. If a congregation is to succeed in achieving green building, biblical instructions for creation care need to shared in both educational programs and worship celebrations, and decades of effort in caring for the environment need to be recognized in order to encourage active engagement today. Partnerships between neighboring congregations can inspire local communities to take positive action in support of environmental concerns, accelerate success by learning from others, and create lasting bonds between members of different congregations.

CHAPTER 2

Cultivating Creation Care Consciousness

Cultivating awareness for creation care can open a congregation to the wonder and beauty all around us. The world and its resources are a gift to all of us. We are to use them responsibly, enjoy them, and preserve them in order that all that comes after us can thrive as well. In this chapter I will touch on some ways congregations can tend our earth and share its bounty with others. I will begin by taking a look at the context of creation care. The increasing number of people on the planet directly affects the distribution and use of its natural resources and contributes to the creation of waste. Creation care is, in a primary way, a matter of hospitality. Sharing natural resources and accomodation for waste production such that all people on the planet can thrive is the goal. Comprehensive creation care entails lifestyle changes in our immediate faith communities and individual lives. We need to reconsider some of our unhelpful patterns of consumption and waste production. Two concepts, *ecological footprint* and *life-cycle costing*, are potential aids to assessing and altering our lifestyle choices. In addition, education and worship are two important avenues through which congregations can promote, build, and celebrate creation care consciousness in community.

POPULATION GROWTH AND HOSPITALITY

The past one hundred years have seen unprecedented population growth in the world. The growth of the human population is a natural process, but demand for natural resources to address the needs of growing communities has also risen. Ever-increasing needs for food, clothing, shelter, transportation, and consumer products creates competition for limited supplies. And those with more financial resources and power tend to acquire a disproportionate volume of available resources. Communities of faith need to consider the role they might play in modeling what is required of a good neighbor, one who seeks the best for the other as well as oneself.

Producers of the public television and online program NOVA have developed a graph of human population growth from the year 0 CE to 2050 CE.[1] According to the presentation, the population of the planet was estimated to be about 300 million in the year 0 CE. At the end of the first millennium, the population was estimated to have reached 310 million, only 10 million people more after one thousand years. By the year 1800, the population hit one billion. China, India, and Europe showed the most significant growth during this period. Gradual developments in science and technology during the second millennium culminated in industrial revolutions from the nineteenth century forward. The world's population grew exponentially with improvements in social organization; the production, storage, and distribution of agricultural products; advances in medicine; exploitation of nonrenewable energy resources (such as coal, natural gas, and oil); and mass production.

In 1927, just 127 years after 1800, the population of the world doubled to two billion. By 1960, only thirty-three years later, the population was three billion. Since then the world population reached four billion in 1974, five billion in 1987, six billion in 1999, and seven billion in 2011. Continuing improvements to our quality of life and natural growth patterns have contributed to this dramatic, rapid growth. Growth patterns today are not equally distributed, however. Many developed countries (for example, the United States, Canada, Russia, Japan, and many European countries) experience lower population growth. Most of the growth is being realized in the developing world (especially Latin America, Africa, and south Asia). An interesting wrinkle is also developing, however. As economic prosperity increases in various countries, population rates are beginning to slow. The predictions of pure exponential growth that were once imagined are being modulated by economic, social, and political variables. Nevertheless, it is projected that if current trends continue, the world will have nine billion people by 2050.

Population growth is significant for creation care because the more people on the planet, the more natural resources that are needed to feed, clothe, and house them. Technological advancements in the past two hundred years have allowed us to acquire and distribute resources globally—but not equitably. Countries that have the most developed infrastructure and highest economic prosperity are using a disproportionate amount of resources relative to their overall populations (see the "Discovering Our Environmental Footprints" section below). When developed countries consume natural resources at a disproportionate rate, they both deprive other people of resources and use up resources faster than they can be replaced—assuming they can be replaced.[2] The inequitable and unsustainable patterns of resource consumption can lead to the oppression of people, increased conflict between groups (due to scarcity of supplies or resentment that some people have more than others or both), and environmental damage.

Attention to the world population trend is important if people of faith are to understand the need to work toward equitable sharing of our natural resources and achieve sustainable patterns of living. The interconnectedness and interdependency of our world no longer allows us to live with the illusion that our acts affect only us as individuals. Given an understanding of the earth as a gift to humanity and the value that God places on *all* people, faith communities ought to view creation care as a fundamental opportunity to pursue hospitality in the world. Our life choices have a real bearing on how people live in the present and will manage in the future. Creation care is an extension of the justice and renewal God would have faith communities pursue and model as his people.

Discovering Our Environmental Footprints

As the population of the planet increases, the material resource demands we make increase, as does the quantity of waste we produce. All people need some level of provision for food, water, clothing, and shelter. Generally speaking, people with more disposable income and more leisure time consume more material resources. For example, human transport systems can shift from reliance on walking or bicycling to communal transport (buses or trains), to individually owned motorized transport (automobiles or motorcycles). Increasing amounts of natural resources and waste are produced with each shift, especially if the infrastructure for supporting each system is considered. Similar trends occur with respect to the proliferation and distribution of consumer products (such as furniture, appliances, tools, televisions, telephones, or computers). The higher the disposable income, the more natural resources required to produce, distribute, and maintain those products, and the more waste in the production, distribution, and disposal of those products.

Our natural human inclination is to indulge ourselves, and we often fail to consider the consequences our lifestyle has on the world's resources and its inhabitants. In US culture today we often make decisions considering only the short term. Our advertising industry frequently accents concern for the immediate when enticing consumers to make a particular purchase. We are conditioned to focus on satisfying immediate impulses or desires, ignoring the environmental consequences of our consumption. For example, we often do not consider the rate at which natural resources are consumed, the waste associated with manufacturing processes, or the end destination of products once their usefulness has ended.

Similar observations could be made about congregations' decisions regarding their buildings. Plans to renovate or build are often focused on the needs of the faith community without much consideration of the environmental consequences of choices about land management and facility creation, alteration, or maintenance. According to the United States Green Building Council (a not-for-profit organization seeking to promote environmental stewardship), buildings in the United States account for the following national patterns:

- 72 percent of electricity consumption
- 39 percent of energy use
- 38 percent of all carbon dioxide emissions
- 40 percent of raw materials use
- 14 percent of potable water consumption
- 30 percent of waste output[3]

These statistics illustrate the fact that our buildings have a significant, ongoing impact on the natural environment. Churches and synagogues often contribute to these consumption and waste patterns. Green building practices could reap significant benefits, however. Environmental benefits include protecting ecosystems, improving air and water quality, reducing solid waste production, and conserving natural resources. Economic benefits include reducing operating costs, enhancing asset value and profits, improving productivity and satisfaction, and optimizing economic performance over the life cycle of a building. Health benefits include improving air, thermal, and acoustic environments; enhancing occupant comfort and health; lessening the strain on local infrastructure; and contributing to overall quality of life in the community.[4]

We need to measure our consumption and waste production on the earth if we are to understand our present impact, develop motivation to change our behaviors, and determine whether our patterns of living are creation friendly. In the early 1990s, the concept of *ecological footprint* began to emerge in academic circles. An ecological footprint attempts to measure the human demand on the resources of the earth. The consumption and waste patterns connected to food, goods, services, housing, and energy are estimated in relation to a particular country, city, or person. Research is conducted to determine variables such as the amount of crop acreage, pastureland, forest area, energy and fresh water resources, and seafood that would be needed to meet consumption demands. A general measure of land and water resources required to meet waste needs is then determined. A primary goal of making estimates of this sort is to determine the earth's ability to sustain various patterns of consumption and to absorb the resulting waste. Generally, the ecological footprint of people in developed countries such as the United States, Canada, and the nations of Europe is larger or heavier than that of people in developing countries (meaning that more land and water resources are required by developed countries than the countries actually possess, which indicates an unsustainable rate of consumption and waste production).

People in developed countries usually have more income per person, increased access to goods and services, and more accumulated material wealth. Larger amounts of the earth's resources can thus be secured to fulfill higher demand for a multitude of products and services. Larger amounts of waste are produced through this consumption cycle. The net result is a more dramatic impact or footprint on the environment.

Although models for calculating an estimated environmental footprint produce varying results, current estimates indicate that if everyone in the world consumed resources and produced waste at the level people in the United States do, sustaining the world's current population would take roughly one and one-third earths.[5] Developing nations use fewer resources and produce less waste, so their consumption and waste production patterns are well within the earth's limits. When the patterns of developed and developing nations are combined, however, our natural resource consumption and waste production exceed the earth's limits. That is, they occur at an unsustainable pace.

The concept of ecological footprint is useful for two reasons: (1) It makes us aware of the wider impact our levels of consumption and waste production have on the world's natural capacities; (2) it suggests ways to alter our lifestyles so that our choices are more sustainable. Calculation tools are available for helping congregations grasp the impact people are having on the environment. Examples of websites that provide resources for exploring the concept of ecological footprints include Redefining Progress (www.myfootprint.org) and Global Footprint Network (www.footprintnetwork.org). Education materials available at these websites will help congregations interpret and apply their findings. The Church of England has launched a National Environmental Campaign that also includes a footprint audit tool (www.shrinkingthefootprint.cofe.anglican.org). Ecological footprint science is fairly new. It is not perfect. But it can help us understand how our individual and communal behaviors are affecting the natural world and suggest ways we can care for creation.

NATIONAL ACTION FOR
ENVIRONMENTAL STEWARDSHIP

We may think creation care is a temporary concern or passing fad. Population growth trends and the increasing demands of people around the planet indicate that the concern is urgent, however. It is also longstanding. In fact, concern for natural resources has been a national agenda item for about one-half the lifespan of the United States. Environmental consciousness entered the imagination of the general public in the United States in the last half of the nineteenth century and grew throughout the early decades of the twentieth century. The need for natural resources conservation came to national prominence in 1871 with the establishment of the United States Commission on Fish and Fisheries. A decline in food fishes such as salmon provoked this effort. Additional agencies concerned with the conservation of birds and mammals were established in later years. Multiple agencies were merged under the US Fish and Wildlife Service in 1940. These efforts focused on caring for these natural, renewable resources and using them in a sustainable way.

Growing environmental consciousness led to the establishment of Yellowstone National Park (the first designated national park in the world) in 1872. The wonders of this area were recognized as a national treasure by our nation's leaders and were set aside for protected use. Figures such as naturalist and writer John Muir (1838–1914) played an important role in the early national conservation effort. Muir's work led to the establishment of Sequoia and Yosemite National Parks in 1890. Building on this momentum, thirteen national forests were set aside by President Grover Cleveland in 1897. Particular federally controlled land, water, minerals, trees, plants, and wildlife were protected through these early efforts, and agencies were created to manage them. In 1905 the United States Forest Service (USFS) was established, and today it manages approximately 193 million acres of forest.[6] The United States National Park Service (USNPS) was established in 1916. Today it manages 394 national parks (as well as historic structures and landmarks, natural landmarks, and wilderness areas) encompassing some eighty-four million acres of land.[7]

The actions of the US federal government have inspired similar conservation around the world. These efforts reflect the recognition that human populations can endanger natural resources. Conservation efforts alone will only prolong the deterioration of the world, however, if they are not accompanied by sustainable patterns of living (patterns of consumption and waste production that can be maintained in the natural world). They can inspire us to consider our local context and discern how our immediate natural resources can be tended as the gift God originally intended.

Supporting national, state, and local environmental stewardship efforts could help congregations become familiar with their immediate physical environment. Our lifestyles today often keep us fairly disconnected from knowledge about the land, water, plants, and wildlife all around us. Regional and local nature centers, farms, natural history museums, and science centers can help us become more aware of the land formations, soil composition, water sources, weather conditions (including rain patterns to guide our water use and solar and wind patterns that affect possible alternative energy potential), and native plants and animals. As we learn about these components, we become aware of the intimate relationship between our local habitat and us. Examining our relationship with the nonhuman creation will yield a clearer understanding of living in harmony with the creation.

RENEWING AN ECOLOGICAL FOCUS

The contemporary study of ecology emerged in the wake of observations from botanists and naturalists in the eighteenth and nineteenth centuries. As natural resources were being set aside for preservation, scientists were discovering relationships between plant, animal, and human populations. Ecologists today examine plants and animals and their habitats. Existing life forms, population numbers, environmental conditions, and the ways in which these life forms interact in a given setting all fall within the purview of ecologists. Their work can expose the wonder of natural interdependency and uncover the unintended negative consequences of human activities. For example, Rachel Carson (1907–1964), a biologist and writer, did much to sensitize her audience to the beauty and mystery of ocean life. Her research, presented in a popular form in the book *Silent Spring* in 1962, exposed the contamination of wildlife and the human food supply through the agricultural use of pesticides such as DDT. Carson can be thought of a catalyst for renewed interest in the field of ecology in the mid-twentieth century.

Carson's work helped to generate momentum for establishing national guidelines for comprehensive environmental protection.[8] In 1970 the Environmental Protection Agency (EPA) was established in the United States. The Clean Air Act (1970), Federal Environmental Pesticide Control Act (1972), Clean Water Act (1972), Noise Control Act (1972), and Endangered Species Act (1973) are examples of policies that were passed shortly after the development of the EPA. The agency also addressed the handling of hazardous materials (for example, related to nuclear energy development) and solid waste disposal. And a host of additional federal acts have been developed up to our present day in an effort to fine-tune previous policies and address new dimensions of environmental degradation.

Our society acknowledges that human activities are affecting our natural world in destructive ways and is quite aware of the acute need for wise environmental stewardship. The health of humanity and its enjoyment of our natural world have been central to the conservation and ecological efforts pursued on a national level. Individual states have developed agencies and legislation to pursue the goals of national environmental policies as well. Faith communities have an established and sympathetic context in which to pursue creation care.

Congregations can contact local environmental organizations to learn about governmental efforts to implement creation care. Tours of local power plants, recycling facilities, wastewater treatment plants, and waste disposal facilities help people understand the impact of our community on the land, air, and water around us as well as help us understand the complexity of coexisting in healthy ways with our environment. Our engagement with existing environmental efforts also alerts us to financial incentives that have been generated by agencies to encourage people to action in their community. Visit the Database of State Incentives for Renewables and Efficiency at www.dsireusa.org for current examples. Energy suppliers and those who distribute environmentally friendly products and services are usually helpful in identifying financial incentives as well.

LIFE-CYCLE THINKING

Financial costs are usually an important factor for congregations to consider when renovating or creating new buildings for worship and ministry. Wise stewardship practices necessitate concern for the costs associated with developing land and buildings. Prioritizing creation care introduces an important dimension to the financial equation, however. In the last twenty years or so, a holistic way of thinking about building costs has emerged in architectural circles. A comprehensive calculation of the expenses related to a building is determined in a model called *life-cycle costing.*

Frequently, we calculate short-term, up-front costs and use them to govern our daily purchasing activities. For example, it is easy to consider the initial cost of a printer for a computer and yet not explore the ongoing costs associated with the ink, toner, or drum that may be required at regular intervals in order to use the product. The purchase price of the printer might be low while ongoing costs for using and maintaining the product over its life span may be high. Wise financial stewardship considers costs associated with long-term use. When environmental stewardship is important to us, we also consider the costs of the materials required to manufacture the printer, the costs of the energy required to power it, and the eventual destination of the printer when it is no longer useful. A holistic vision of creation care includes financial and environmental considerations over the life cycle of a product, from birth to reuse. (In a completely sustainable world reuse would be the goal for everything we use.)

Life-cycle thinking is necessary if congregations are to care for creation through their property and buildings. Purchasing the least expensive property and building materials does not necessarily achieve the goals of either financial or environmental stewardship. In fact, such impulses often contribute to unsustainable patterns of living and significant financial costs in the long term. Congregations need to expand their vision to include start-up costs, long-term operations and maintenance, and ultimate reuse or deconstruction. Environmental and financial stewardship are interconnected, and all phases of a product's or building's life should be considered.

For example, site selection presents us with opportunities and challenges. Is it better to build on a developed site or an undeveloped site? Developed sites might allow us to reclaim resources. Previously occupied land often requires less site preparation and can be developed in ways that restore its health and beauty.

Reusing existing buildings or recycling materials into a new building on the developed site can minimize the use of natural resources, diminish waste, and preserve architectural treasures. Use of existing sites may lessen the impact of urban sprawl as well, allowing for more open and natural spaces. I am not arguing against the use of undeveloped sites so much as trying to provoke new questions for congregations. Undeveloped sites can provide congregations with numerous ways to express thoughtful creation care, but some communities may occupy or purchase developed sites that could exhibit a profound gesture of stewardship.

Once a site is selected, how should it be developed? What natural habitat surrounds the site? Are there land features, plants, and wildlife indigenous to the site and surrounding area that could be preserved? Studying the ecology of the congregational site will build a connection to the immediate environment, cultivate natural beauty, and assist with building design choices. Attention to solar and wind patterns can uncover potential for natural lighting, heating, and cooling or even help determine the availability of alternative energy sources. Attention to rainfall, and its natural collection and dispersion, can influence decisions about storm-water management, water reuse, and landscaping choices. Use of existing and indigenous plantings can help with energy costs (by shading of some parts of the building), minimize landscape maintenance costs, and also assist with storm-water management.

Building material choices become more complex when viewed from a life-cycle perspective. Initial cost is no longer the ruling factor for selection. The origin of the product, its composition, and its potential for reuse become important. Origin matters in that selecting local products can reduce the energy costs associated with long-distance transportation and contribute to the economic viability of the local community. Those concerned about composition promote the use of renewable resources, the elimination of toxic substances that may harm building occupants, and long-term durability. And costs are inevitably generated when disposing of building materials that are no longer useful for their original purpose. Responsible stewardship also includes considering the ultimate reuse of buildings and their constituent parts. Selecting products that can be used again for their original purpose or re-cycled into other products is necessary for comprehensive creation care.

Energy acquisition and use is central to creation care. Congregational buildings require energy for lighting, heating, cooling, ventilation, food preparation, office activities, and running electrical devices of all kinds, and we should use the most durable, highest efficiency energy-consuming products we can. Lowest price for products in the short term often translates into long-term costs related to durability and energy consumption. With the increasing price of energy today, higher initial investment in energy-efficient products can rapidly be recovered in reduced energy use costs. Congregations also need to explore alternative energy production potential. Windmills and photovoltaic panels and cells (harnessing solar energy) can supplement other energy sources in many parts of the country. The very location of the building affects the expenditure of energy as well. Locating our buildings in or near urban centers or mass transit lines, connecting with pedestrian or bicycle access routes, and making provision for clean energy transportation will all contribute to responsible long-term energy use.

In addition, emission of greenhouse gases, gases that retain heat in the atmosphere, needs to be factored into a life-cycle vision of building as creation care. Carbon dioxide, methane, nitrous oxide, and fluorinated gases are the primary greenhouse gases,[9] and their presence contributes to elevating the temperature of the environment around the planet. Human beings and a variety of biological processes naturally produce carbon dioxide. Various manufacturing processes and the burning of fossil fuels (oil, natural gas, and coal), solid waste, and trees and wood products also produce carbon dioxide. Plants absorb carbon dioxide, but the existing vegetation of the earth can absorb only so much. When the amount of gas produced exceeds plants' capacity to absorb carbon dioxide, the gas builds up in the atmosphere. The increasing human population, need for energy, and manufacturing production around the world all contribute to higher levels of carbon dioxide production. The Fourth US Climate Action Report indicates that carbon dioxide emissions increased by 20 percent from 1990 to 2004.[10] The buildup of carbon dioxide in the atmosphere accelerates rising temperatures around our planet, a phenomenon called global warming. Global warming has multiple environmental consequences, some of which are harmful to life. Support for forest preservation is due, in part, to the recognized need to encourage the natural processing of carbon dioxide, but communities themselves, including congregations, need to develop a long-term vision for reducing greenhouse gas emissions. Promoting the use of renewable or recycled local resources for building materials, high-efficiency energy products, passive energy sources, indigenous landscaping, and the transportation systems that eliminate or reduce the burning of fossil fuels will all help to combat the production and buildup of greenhouse gases.

The issue of global warming has generated some debate in the world today. It is true that our earth experiences natural warming and cooling cycles over the course of time. The rapid increase in global temperature of the last thirty years can likely be attributed, in part, to a natural warming trend. But seven billion people who consume natural resources and produce waste do have an impact on the planet's atmosphere as well. The measurements of the gases noted above are real and are, in part, also altering global temperature. While we cannot change natural warming and cooling cycles, we can alter the quantity of gas emissions related to human activities.

Population pressures, patterns of resource use and waste production, conservation efforts, and ecological awareness all come to bear on life-cycle thinking. As increases in economic development in many rapidly growing areas such as India and China are realized, the competition for resources will increase, as will the production of waste. Faith communities have a wonderful opportunity to model life-cycle visioning as an expression of creation care that minimizes natural resource consumption and waste production, maximizes energy use, and harmonizes with the immediate locale, natural and human built.

GUIDES FOR "GREENING" CONGREGATIONS

Education is essential to developing creation care to its fullest potential in congregational settings. The many websites and associated materials noted at the end of chapter 1 and in Appendix A will provide a plethora of sources from which to develop excellent curriculum, programs, and other initiatives for people of all ages. Young people represent an especially powerful catalyst for change in the life of every congregation. Their high level of energy, willingness to try new approaches, and optimism can empower creation care across the community. Engaging them in creation care will both stimulate the larger congregation and help to train the upcoming generation in making sustainable life choices.

A number of guides to help congregations learn about greening their buildings and property are available. A handful of representative interreligious, interdenominational, denominational, and congregation-based materials illustrate the range of resources for green building. Each of the guides noted here is available as a free, downloadable file via the Internet.

Greening Sacred Spaces Health and Sustainability Guide: A Daily Operations Guide for Faith Communities (no date)[11] is produced by Faith and the Common Good, an interreligious organization based in Cambridge, Ontario. This guide emerged from a Greening Sacred Spaces program they initiated in 2003. The guide provides environmental facts, tips for green building strategies, and vendors of environmentally friendly products. Many of the vendors included are based in Ontario, appropriate for promoting developing local and regional supply networks (a green building strategy in and of itself). Cleaning and maintaining a building is addressed as well. Additional resources are provided at the website, including a booklet with suggestions for developing creation care leadership, brief profiles of how some congregations have implemented greening their buildings, and materials for promoting ecospirituality in a congregational setting.

The Green Faith Guide: Working Together to Protect and Restore Our Environment (2004) is distributed by the District of Columbia Energy Office.[12] *The Green Faith Guide* was developed in collaboration with religious communities of many kinds, including Jewish, Muslim, Christian, Baha'i, Unitarian Universalist, Buddhist, and Sikh. A different author has written each of the fifteen chapters. Short chapters touch on the following building issues: designing green buildings, landscaping and gardening, water and energy use, waste, and paying for green initiatives. Mention is made of the US Green Building Council's Leadership in Energy and Environmental Design (LEED) rating program, which will be discussed in detail in chapter 3. Additional resources for congregational education are included as well. Numerous organizations and networks are mentioned in the final pages of the document, many of which are especially relevant to the Washington, DC, region. A guide of this type builds on shared faith values that religious communities can unite around to achieve and model creation care together.

Rejoice in Your Handiwork: Sacred Space and Synagogue Architecture (2005)[13] and the "Room by Room Greening Guide" (no date)[14] have been developed by the Union for Reform Judaism. "Part One: Congregational Guide to the Process of Renovating and Building" addresses many important initial issues such as mobilizing the congregation for a renovation or building project, determining budgets and fund-raising, exploring options for expanding or remaining in existing facilities, and working with the architect and other professionals. "Part Two: Form and Function: Design Considerations for Congregations" contains many short articles on multiple issues related to faith, worship, and built environments. Many excellent examples of contemporary synagogue design are presented throughout this volume. Environmental stewardship issues are discussed in two articles toward the end of the collection. Congregation Beth David (San Luis Sustainability Group), San Luis Obispo, California, is featured as an example of green design. Specific green design choices of Congregation Beth David are noted in the first article, "Conservation and Sustainability." Congregation Beth David will be featured in detail later in this book. The second article, "Building Health and Personal Well-Being," addresses the importance of interior environmental health. The majority of the guide addresses more general building concerns, but creation care is highlighted. The Room by Room Greening Guide is composed of seven one-page lists that suggest particular dimensions of building projects. Brief remarks and a checklist of items to consider for the greening of architecture in general—the bathroom, the classroom, commuting, gardens, the kitchen, and office space—have been prepared.

Building a Firm Foundation: A Creation-Friendly Building Guide for Churches (2006) has been developed by the National Council of Churches USA through their Eco-Justice Program Office.[15] The thirty-page guide mentions the LEED program as a useful tool for seeking to design in a sustainable way. Suggestions concerning site selection and development, building materials, energy and water considerations, landscaping, and transportation are included. Several pages of useful websites are found at the end of the document.

The *Green Shalom Action Guide* (2006) is an example of a local congregation sharing its journey and resources for creation care with others.[16] Temple Emanuel, Kensington, Maryland, under the leadership of Rabbi Warren G. Stone, developed this guide as a tool to encourage all of its families to implement creation care in their daily lives. Temple Emanuel will be featured later in this book. The guide contains inspirational readings, a history of the congregation's green activities, recommended actions, and resources to consult for further growth and action. Building and property issues are addressed throughout the document. The guide concludes with the environmental policy statement of the congregation. Regular energy audits of the buildings; comprehensive landscaping plans, including a biblically inspired garden; recycling programs and cleaning products; and green strategies for the disposal of waste, among many other goals, are discussed here. The guide encourages applying the congregation's model in the homes of the people. It is impressive to see an individual congregation articulate, celebrate, and envision ongoing creation care in this way.

The *Environmental Guide for Congregations, Their Buildings, and Grounds* (2006), edited by David Glover and David Rhoads, is available through the website for Web of Creation.[17] The materials in the guide provide worship resources, environmental facts, and concrete suggestions for minimizing a congregation's impact on the earth. Sections address a variety of important topics, including water, energy, transportation, food choices, cleaning products, indoor air quality, and waste. References to additional resources are included in every section.

The Greening Guide (2007) is available through the United Jewish Appeal (UJA) Federation of New York as a part of their Network Greening Initiative.[18] Suggestions for implementing green building principles abound in the document. Sections include viable greening options (for example, examining energy and water use, air quality, waste, and cleaning), greening interior and exterior spaces, new construction (mention is made of the LEED rating system), and facilities management. One section is devoted to environmental resource information especially for those in the greater New York City area. Other sections address financial incentives for pursuing greening initiatives and independent certification programs that verify the environmental claims of manufacturers (certification programs are discussed in chapter 3). Many website links and publications relevant to environmental care in general are also included.

The *Green Sanctuary Manual* (2009) was prepared by the Unitarian Universalist Association of Congregations (UUA).[19] The manual, first published in 1991 as the *Green Sanctuary Handbook*, promotes a denominational program that seeks to create "Green Sanctuaries" throughout the country. Congregations are invited to participate in activities that demonstrate creation care and can apply to be officially recognized for their commitment to being green. In June 2011, 171 accredited Green Sanctuary congregations had been recognized and 108 congregations were in candidacy process (the total representing 25 percent of the congregations in the UUA). Worship and celebration, religious education, environmental justice, and sustainable living are the four focus areas to be pursued by each congregation. Examples of ways to address each area are presented throughout the manual. Sustainable living sections highlight issues related to the building and property. (Homes are emphasized in addition to the religious community buildings.) Chapters touch on landscaping, water and energy, waste, cleaning, and maintenance issues. Additional resources are noted near the end of the manual along with a list of denominational environmental statements. The overall approach of the manual is quite integrated and could offer faith communities some helpful ideas for developing creation care consciousness and for considering tangible projects.

INTEGRATION INTO WORSHIP LIFE

Raising awareness of the need for creation care and implementing concrete changes to our lifestyle patterns is facilitated by including references to environmental stewardship in worship celebrations. Regularly setting aside a season or special days in the worship life of our congregations to accent the beauty of the world around us and to recognize the abundance of resources given to us by the Creator is a pattern of creation care worth considering. In the busyness of life, we sometimes forget about the profound beauty that surrounds us in the people we encounter from day to day, in the landscapes we occupy, and in the flora and fauna that grace the planet. Calling attention to the beauty of the creation may give us pause to thank our God for gifts that dazzle the eye and inspire the spirit.

In conjunction with acknowledging creation's beauty, we can praise God for the abundance of natural resources that fuel our lifestyles. Air, water, and land—all necessary for life as we know it—often go unrecognized. All are essential for our very existence. The manufacturing of biological and geological materials into products that feed, clothe, shelter, and transport us often goes unnoticed. It is easy to take the world's abundance for granted when we live in a land of plenty. Thanking God for provision beyond our imagining and actual need is a necessary prelude to our changing our lifestyle choices.

The superabundance of goods and services we have in the United States, Canada, and many developed nations often makes us oblivious to our human tendency to covet possessions and indulge in excess. To be human is to struggle with selfishness. "Not quite enough" is an impression we often have as we consider portion sizes of food, the square footage of our houses, expansion of our wardrobe, levels of income, and the number of objects we acquire for entertainment. Our resistance to limits and our lack of contentment lead us into patterns for living that affect other people in the world and the creation itself in destructive ways. In addition to confronting our insatiable appetite for more, we must recognize the substantial impact such an orientation achieves. Our praise in worship needs to be accompanied by repenting of our consuming too much and producing too much waste.

In our worship, we need to acknowledge the destructive consequences of pursuing our self-interest. The issue here is not that humanity uses the natural resources of the earth but the degree to which a relatively small portion of humanity acquires, processes, and consumes those resources. Unintended consequences have surely resulted from our self-indulgent patterns of living. Confessing the wrongs of this way of life is important if we are to achieve a true change of heart. A number of communities have begun to make this type of confession in their regular corporate prayers.

We can become agents of reconciliation in the wake of our public confessions. It is one thing to acknowledge and confess sin; it is another to take concrete steps to renew the brokenness that has resulted. To seek reconciliation is to act as a redemptive agent on God's behalf. People of faith have the opportunity to become conduits of reconciliation through creation care activities. Created in the image of God, we can become agents of God's grace at work in the world today. We can move our creation care from good intentions to tangible achievements in pursuing an active response to confession.

In recent years, particular days for marking environmental care have been embraced. In 1970 approximately twenty million people celebrated Earth Day for the first time in the United States, and April 22 has been designated for the observance. Many faith communities orient worship services near this date to recognize the divine gift of creation and humanity's responsibilities to care for it. Worship resources for Earth Day (or alternative days upon which to recognize environmental stewardship) may be found via the National Religious Partnership for the Environment website. The National Council of Churches of Christ Eco-Justice Programs website has links to Earth Day and other worship materials. A number of worship resources (suggestions for prayers, songs, biblical texts, sermon ideas, and related materials) are available through denominational websites as well.

In Jewish communities materials are produced for the service of *Tu B'Shvat* (the Jewish New Year of the Trees). Tu B'Shvat is a holiday celebrated on the fifteenth of the month of Shvat in the Jewish calendar, which usually falls in the last half of January to early February in the Gregorian calendar. Emphases similar to Earth Day are included in these services. The website for the Coalition on the Environment and Jewish Life has links to resources for Tu B'Shvat and Earth Day. A page on the website, "Celebrate: The Jewish Holidays," provides links to resources that can assist congregations in accenting creation care through these events and on Rosh Hashanah and Yom Kippur, Sukkoth, Hanukkah, Purim, Passover, Shavuot, and Shabbat. (On the website, www.coejl.org/index.php, click on "Resources," then "Links," then "Celebrate.") Dimensions of creation care are implicit in primary holiday services, and highlighting them for worshipers can serve as a formational avenue through which to cultivate responsible stewardship of the earth.

CONCLUSIONS

Creation care consciousness can be nurtured in our congregations by acknowledging environmental realities and choosing to alter our lifestyles. I have noted the exponential growth of the human population to indicate that we have an immediate, unprecedented opportunity to become more hospitable world neighbors. The concept of ecological footprints will help us measure our impact on the planet. We can see where our present rates of consumption and waste production stand today and adjust our lifestyles in ways that will be responsible (to serve and protect) and hospitable to human and nonhuman neighbors. Our understanding of the earth as a gift to be treasured can be translated into preserving, conserving, and responsibly using its many resources.

The greening of our congregations will require a long-term educational commitment to creation care and regular integration of creation-oriented themes into our worship. An increasing number of print and media resources, workshops, camps, and community initiatives are emerging from faith-based sources to encourage wise environmental stewardship. And the worship of God provides a rich and powerful arena in which to celebrate creation care. We can offer praise and thanks for the beauty and bounty of the earth, confess our failure to consider the consequences of indulgent behavior, and act to bring about healing and generosity.

CHAPTER 3

Green Synagogue and Church Building as Creation Care

Designing, constructing, and maintaining buildings in ways that are good for the health of the human community and the natural world is often described as *green* or *sustainable*. Greening the built environment of a faith community is a powerful way to achieve and model a commitment to creation care. An increasing number of congregations across the country are greening their churches and synagogues, either through the choices they make from the beginning of a new project or through gradual, systematic upgrades to existing facilities. This chapter will begin by examining the levels of sustainability that can be pursued under the designation "green building," followed by a glimpse of the status of green building today. Certification, Energy Star, Interfaith Power and Light, and Leadership in Energy and Environmental Design (LEED) programs will be examined as four resources to assist congregations with green building. And historical preservation will be highlighted to illustrate that green building can be achieved in all building arenas, old and new.

A Spectrum of Green Building

Prior to the 1990s, conventional modern building was largely focused on function, comfort, and cost. Aesthetic considerations may or may not have been a significant emphasis, depending on who designed the project and the willingness of the client to invest in beauty. Conventional building did not usually concern itself with minimizing site disturbance or waste production, scarcity of source materials, the specific content or geographic origin of building materials, consuming resources such as water or energy, or maximizing interior air quality. At its worst, maximizing square footage and minimizing cost became the overriding factors driving conventional design. Cultural impulses to consume the earth's resources without regard for consequences fueled this approach.

Acknowledgement of the physical limitations of the world and the impact of humanity on the planet, discussed in chapter 2, is encouraging the gradual transformation from a conventional approach to a green approach. Green building is a good alternative to conventional building, but can have a spectrum of goals. A modest goal is to increase efficiency in the building industry and in the functioning of buildings. This would include producing building materials more efficiently and creating higher performing products. One step beyond higher efficiency design is seeking to achieve zero impact on the environment. This would include increasing efficiency in production and performance, conserving resources, and limiting waste production to levels that could be absorbed naturally by the environment. Sustainable design, that is, using resources and producing waste at rates that could be maintained perpetually, is the goal of this level of green building. The focus of these first two goals is identifying the best technological solutions that can be developed while maintaining cost effectiveness. Human use, comfort, cost, and aesthetics, to some degree, remain ultimate concerns.

Two additional levels of green building go beyond sustainability. Human concerns are important to these levels, but the natural world becomes a more significant partner for design as well. In their book, *The Integrative Design Guide to Green Building*, authors 7group (a multidisciplinary group of professionals dedicated to sustainable design—John Boecker, Scot Horst, Tom Keiter, Andrew Lau, Marcus Sheffer, and Brian Toevs) and Bill Reed identify these levels as "restorative" and "regenerative."[1] The goal of restorative design is to restore a natural environment to a state of self-perpetuating health. This goal takes the needs of the natural habitat to heart and seeks to create buildings in ways that will promote health for both human and nonhuman life. Regenerative design seeks to conceive of ways to build in a natural world that not only cooperate with nature but also encourage ongoing learning and mutually beneficial change. The difference between restorative and regenerative design is perhaps slight. It may help to think of the goal of restorative design as more static (a fixed, specified level of health) and the goal of regenerative design as more dynamic (an open-ended, ever-improving level of thriving). Restorative and regenerative goals for green building require consideration of design concerns beyond mere high efficiency or human sustainability.

For communities of faith, pursuing green building is a process of growing understanding, unfolding commitment, and gradual achievement. As we enter the world of greening our spaces for worship and ministry we may seek higher efficiency products and improve our consumption rate of natural resources through conservation (although nonrenewable resources will still disappear one day). Changing to high efficiency light bulbs, recycling our paper plates, and using low-flow water fixtures is a start, but much, much more is required to be truly wise and faithful stewards. If we take the admonitions of Scripture seriously, we will recognize the significance of restorative and regenerative goals for our building projects. God has designed a remarkable natural world in which to live. We could learn from the diverse world around us, treasure its partnership, and seek to fulfill our biblical charge to serve and protect by embracing the most comprehensive green-building initiatives we can achieve.

GREEN BUILDING TODAY

Green building involves designing and constructing in ways that are environmentally, economically, and socially responsible. Environmental benefits include conservation of natural resources, protection of biodiversity, improved air and water quality, and reduction of waste. Economic benefits include optimizing the performance of the building throughout its life cycle, reducing operating costs, encouraging the local economy, improving productivity for the occupants, and contributing to the development of environmentally sensitive products and services. Social benefits include increased occupant health and comfort, minimized strain on the local infrastructure, improved overall quality of life, and enhanced aesthetic qualities of the building and its site.[2] Our efforts at creation care through green building manifest a host of benefits consistent with biblical values and priorities.

Green building considers dimensions of a project from its inception to its reuse or demise. Sometimes addressing the entire life cycle of the building is called a "whole building" approach. A long-term, comprehensive vision is charted to guide the siting of the structure, design, construction, operation, maintenance, renovation, and deconstruction.[3] The natural setting for the project is considered. Efforts are made to disturb the land as little as possible, work with the natural contours and features, and directionally orient the building(s) to maximize energy use. The indigenous beauty and biodiversity of the natural setting is maintained or restored. When a developed site is utilized for building, attention is focused on maximizing the recycling of materials and reducing waste from the project.

Materials are selected with care in green building, with priority given to renewable and recycled resources as well as those that are durable and the least toxic (ideally, nontoxic) to life. Interior environments are carefully planned to incorporate ample natural light, encourage natural ventilation, and achieve optimal air quality. Minimizing energy and water consumption is paramount.

High-efficiency technologies and conservation strategies are used. Renewable energy sources are incorporated into the design as is possible and appropriate. Materials that require minimal transportation to the site are selected, both for the way in which this minimizes energy expenditures as building materials are moved to a site and for the economic benefits to local and regional manufacturers. Designers seek to encourage pedestrian traffic and mass transit access. The ultimate purpose of green building is to create environments that are life giving for the human occupants and the natural world.

In the history of architecture, formal and informal, structures built by people have often capitalized on the beauty and material resources of the natural world. For example, artifacts of some indigenous people of the Americas demonstrate that observations of the seasons and changes in temperature and light cycles have influenced the orientation of the building, choice of building materials based on local renewable resources, the location and number of openings for natural light and air flow, and use of natural insulating materials (such as earth or plant materials). Green building is not really new. But development of modern building materials and techniques, increased costs of energy sources, and the recognition of unintended environmental degradation have precipitated a renewed interest in green building.

The outbreak of "sick building syndrome" across the United States illustrates unintended negative effects of contemporary architecture techniques and materials.[4] Some people experience acute negative health and comfort effects in certain buildings. When the people leave the building in question, their symptoms disappear. Often no precise link to a particular cause can be identified. But the number of complaints and the ongoing nature of the problem indicate something is wrong with these buildings. Indoor air quality is one concern. Thousands of products emit gases called "volatile organic compounds" or VOCs, chemicals that are released over short or long periods of time. Products that emit VOCs include paints, cleaning supplies, office equipment, and building materials and furnishings. Building interiors concentrate VOC emissions. In contemporary building, the combination of materials (such as laminated products, adhesives, surface coatings, upholstery, and carpet), along with the construction technique of conserving energy by sealing buildings, unintentionally raises levels of VOCs. For example, installing windows that can't be opened helps to seal a building, but limits the intake of fresh air. Mechanical heating, cooling, and ventilation systems recirculate the same air and unintentionally contribute to raising levels of VOCs. Green building seeks ecofriendly ways to achieve healthy and comfortable interior environments.

Green building has become more mainstream in our culture in recent decades. The primary professional organization for architects in the United States, the American Institute of Architects (AIA), created a Committee on the Environment (COTE) in 1990. The AIA/COTE has worked at developing and disseminating accurate information concerning green building for and in conjunction with the professional community, the building industry, the scientific community, and the general public. Since 1997 AIA/COTE has selected "Top Ten Green Projects" (see listings and information concerning these featured projects at www.aia.org). In 2009 Jewish Reconstructionist Congregation, Evanston, Illinois, was featured as a top-ten selection and will be explored later in this book.

The AIA/COTE was able to initiate research into green building in 1990 through a grant from the Environmental Protection Agency. This research project led to the development of a guide for the architecture profession aimed at helping architects assess issues of human health and well-being. The *Environmental Resource Guide* (ERG) was released in 1992 and continues to be available as a software product. The regularly updated guide helps architects to see that green building goes beyond simply conforming to a building code. The impact on natural ecosystems from the point of a building's conception to the final phase of reuse or deconstruction is emphasized. Life-cycle cost analysis is featured to encourage maximum economic benefits. Congregations can express creation care through green building by working with professional architects committed to and conversant with green building.

Whole networks of building professionals now exist to share information, products, and services related to green building. The

Sustainable Buildings Industry Council (SBIC) is an independent, nonprofit group committed to promoting sustainable design among architects, engineers, manufacturers, and building associations (www.sbicouncil.org). The SBIC partners with federal agencies, such as the United States General Services Administration (GSA), Environmental Protection Agency, and the Department of Energy (DoE) on sustainable design initiatives. Earlier in this decade they partnered with the Naval Facilities Engineering Command, GSA, Department of Defense, and other federal agencies to create the Whole Building Design Guide (www.wbdg.org). This program emphasizes an integrated design approach that involves the whole building stakeholder community in working toward sustainable objectives. Federal and private sector programs combine their resources and share their knowledge in the pursuit of green building through these channels.

Congregations need to be discerning when engaging green building assistance. The claims of professionals, products, or services proclaiming a commitment to creation care should be verified. Mere affiliation with green networks is not enough. Architects, contractors, consultants, and suppliers need to demonstrate their training and knowledge of green building principles and practices. It is a good idea to talk with former clients of building professionals and to visit nearby synagogues and churches to evaluate the quality of the professional's work and environmental commitment, and to spark ideas for your own congregation.

CERTIFICATION PROGRAMS AND LABELING

To help consumers evaluate a particular manufacturer's sources for raw materials, production processes, and packaging, verification and certification systems are being developed to substantiate and promote sustainable efforts. In the past twenty years or so, a number of independent agencies have emerged to certify compliance with sustainable living standards.

Several organizations have been established to assist us in making wise selections concerning wood, an important renewable building material for synagogues and churches. Wood is used for infrastructure (such as the framing of buildings) and as a finished surface (such as in flooring and furniture). Two issues are important for using this building material in light of creation care. First, planners should select wood and wood products that are indigenous to one's geographic area. Choosing local materials reduces the amount of energy needed to transport products to the building site, builds the economy of the local community, and celebrates the natural resources of the immediate area. Second, planners should encourage sustainable practices in the wood industry itself. As congregations, we have the power to encourage responsible cultivation, management, and manufacturing of wood and wood products. Certification usually verifies the country of origin of the wood and that the lumber company follows sustainable forest management practices. The Forest Stewardship Council (FSC) was established in 1993 as an independent, not-for-profit organization to promote responsible management of the world's forests (www. fsc.org). The FSC has developed standards that companies and organizations can pursue to achieve the FSC seal of compliance. Fifty countries now utilize this internationally recognized standard. Using wood that has FSC certification is a way for us to encourage responsible stewardship of the world's timber resources.

McDonough Braungart Design Chemistry (MBDC) is a company founded in 1995 by William McDonough and Michael Braungart as a product and process design firm seeking to implement ecoeffective principles. McDonough is an architect by training and Braungart a chemist. In 2002 McDonough and Braungart coauthored the book *Cradle to Cradle* to promote their ideas.[5] They identify the ways that we usually build and manufacture today as based on a "take-make-waste" model that emerged with the Industrial Revolution. In contrast to this "cradle-to-grave" paradigm, they promote a "cradle-to-cradle" (C2C) approach to building and manufacturing. Strategies that benefit the whole human community socially, economically, and environmentally become paramount. Such an approach prioritizes reusing existing materials over and over, utilizes renewable energy sources wisely, and ultimately produces only waste that can be reintegrated into our production stream or absorbed in a natural and balanced way by the ecosystem. MBDC has restorative and regenerative goals in mind for its building and manufacturing solutions.

McDonough and Braungart acknowledge that differing local circumstances will usually require unique solutions to production challenges; no singular, universal solution is imagined. They recognize that significant changes to our established patterns will take time to achieve. They emphasize the importance of creativity and pursuit of the common good (the value for the larger community, not just the company or its stockholders).

MBDC has applied its C2C philosophy to architecture and community design services through William McDonough and Partners, Charlottesville, Virginia, and to certification for manufacturing companies and their products. McDonough architectural projects include the Environmental Defense Fund National Headquarters (1985); the Herman Miller GreenHouse Factory and Offices (1995); 901 Cherry Offices for Gap Inc. (1997); Oberlin College's Adam Joseph Lewis Center for Environmental Studies (2000); and the revitalization project of the Ford Rouge Center (ongoing). The buildings designed by MBDC could provide restorative green building models for congregations seeking to embody a high level of sustainability. Manufacturing companies may seek C2C certification for their products at one of four levels: basic, silver, gold, and platinum. Once certification is achieved, the company may display in its product labeling and marketing the logo that corresponds to the certification level achieved.

In December 2009 the Green Products Innovation Institute was established in California to continue to develop and administer cradle-to-cradle certification. The institute is now called the Cradle to Cradle Products Innovation Institute (CCPII; www.c2c-certified.org). CCPII works with partners in the environmental community, education, government, and industry to develop the C2C certification program and administer the certification mark of MBDC. Information concerning C2C-certified building materials, interior design products, paper and packaging, textiles and fabric, and personal and home care products may be found at their website under the "Product Certification" tab. Building products currently listed address building exteriors, façades, composite materials, concrete products, insulation, drywall, and daylighting products. Interior design products address needs for carpeting, ceilings, floor coverings, lighting, furniture for education and offices, and workstation accessories. C2C certification is one of the most comprehensive programs that congregations could choose to support in seeking to promote creation care.

Thousands of manufactured products could be used in congregational building and renovation projects. Discerning compliance with green building values is a significant challenge. Scientific Certification Systems (SCS; www.scscertified.com) was established in the mid-1980s as an independent organization to develop standards and certification of environmental, sustainable, and food quality claims. SCS assesses a company's social actions, energy usage, material selection, and human and ecosystem health impacts. SCS often cooperates with various agencies to certify products useful for congregational projects. Certification programs include the following:

- *Level*: for office furniture systems, components, and seating (www.levelcertified.org); developed in conjunction with the Business and Institutional Furniture Manufacturers Association (BIFMA; www.bifma.org)
- *Indoor Advantage*: for office furniture systems, components, and seating (www.scscertified.com/gbc/indooradvantage.php); developed in conjunction with BIFMA and the US Green Building Council's Leadership in Energy and Environmental Design (LEED) program
- *Indoor Advantage Gold*: for building materials such as adhesives and sealants, paints and coatings, textiles and wall coverings, composite wood, and classroom and office furniture systems; developed in conjunction with the California Office of Environmental Health Hazard Assessment

- *Floorscore*: for hard surface flooring and flooring adhesives; developed in conjunction with the Resilient Floor Covering Institute (www.rfci.com)
- *Recycled Material Content*: includes certification for determination of preconsumer and/or postconsumer recycled content in a product (certified recycled content) and certification of biodegradable liquid products (especially cleaning products)
- *Sustainable Choice*: for carpets and rugs
- *No Formaldehyde*: for composite wood, laminate, and adhesive products
- *Forest Stewardship Council Chain of Custody*: for certifying that FSC standards were met throughout the production process, from forest to consumer

Products conforming to these certification programs are identified with a logo on the product packaging and promotional materials.

Often we remain fairly unaware of the effects the products we encounter each day in our homes, offices, classrooms, or religious spaces have on us and our environment. Use of the SCS assessment programs noted above would help to promote healthy processes for manufacturing and the use of nontoxic, renewable materials and would reduce the number of harmful chemicals used in building products that enhance our congregational spaces. SCS has been working with The Home Depot to evaluate environmental claims appearing on its consumer products as well—a welcome note for those congregations that may use products from this large building supplier. Products found to be in compliance with SCS criteria will be certified and distributed through the Eco Options program.

Green Seal (www.greenseal.org) is another independent, nonprofit organization that verifies the environmental claims of manufacturers. Manufacturers can submit products and services to be tested in accordance with international guidelines for environmental labeling programs. Green Seal lists verified products and services on its website (updated weekly). Some of Green Seal's reports feature products that are not actually certified but merely recommended based on manufacturer's data. (Not all product categories are covered by Green Seal environmental standards.) Green Seal acknowledges that noncertified products or services are only potentially preferable. Discernment is needed in using all verification systems, but special care should be taken to distinguish between certified and noncertified products and services on recommendation lists.

ENERGY STAR PROGRAM

In 1992 the United States Environmental Protection Agency (EPA) created the Energy Star program as a voluntary labeling initiative to identify and promote energy-efficient products. Reducing energy usage saves people money and helps to reduce greenhouse gas emissions generated through the production of energy. Computers, monitors, office equipment, and residential heating and cooling equipment were the first products to be labeled with energy efficiency information between 1992 and 1995. In 1996 the EPA partnered with the US Department of Energy to expand labeling to major appliances, lighting, home electronics, and other energy-consuming devices. Today, information concerning energy-efficient products and energy efficiency in general can be found at www. energystar.gov. Insight into product labeling, home improvement (including tools for energy audits), federal tax credits, and even rebates on products from manufacturers can be found here. A host of partners working with the program can be searched via the website as well.

Of particular interest is a section of the website entitled "Congregations." A thirty-nine-page guide, "Putting Energy into Stewardship: The Energy Star Guide for Congregations," is available as a free PDF document.[6] The guide has information about initiating a project (including locating various kinds of funding), a range of energy-consuming products, ways to calculate savings, and sustainable living (addressing renewable energy, air pollution, new building design, paper use and products, recycling, water, and even the unique demands of megachurches). Nearly fifteen hundred congregations have been recognized as Energy Star Congregations, and some congregations have achieved remarkable energy savings. A list of congregations recognized as award winners for their excellence in energy efficiency going back to 1999 can be found, and an interactive map allows the viewer to locate nearby congregations. The federal government has recognized the leadership congregations can provide for their communities.

INTERFAITH POWER AND LIGHT NETWORK

In 1998 concern over the impact of global warming provided incentive for the Reverend Canon Sally G. Bingham, Grace Cathedral, San Francisco, to found a multiparish effort to educate members about the benefits of energy conservation, to promote energy efficiency, and to combine their influence in seeking the purchase of renewable energy. The initiative was called Episcopal Power and Light. In 2000 the movement was broadened to include additional faith partners under the name California Interfaith Power and Light. Hundreds of congregations in California were mobilized to adopt creation care oriented energy choices and to support legislative efforts to improve climate control and the pursuit of clean energy in their state.

Today the Interfaith Power and Light (IPL) movement is a network of affiliates active in thirty-seven states and the Washington, DC, area (see www.interfaithpowerandlight.org). More than ten thousand congregations participate in the education and efficient and clean energy benefits provided by IPL. The expanding network continues to be a catalyst for shrinking the carbon footprints of congregations and supporting legislation at the state and federal levels in concert with environmental care. Temple Emanuel, Kensington, Maryland, and Pulaski Heights United Methodist Church, Little Rock, Arkansas, congregations featured later in this book, are both active in the IPL movement. Guidelines for forming an affiliate in a state that does not yet have an IPL presence are provided on the website, along with news and resources for congregations.

LEADERSHIP IN ENERGY AND ENVIRONMENTAL DESIGN (LEED)

Multiple rating systems are available to help building professionals measure and document compliance with standardized green building criteria. Some of the larger national systems for homes include EarthCraft, Enterprise Community Partners Green Communities Criteria, National Association of Home Builders Green Building Program, and American Lung Association Healthy Home program. Green Globes and Leadership in Energy and Environmental Design (LEED) are programs that address multiple building types and would apply to congregational building programs.[7] LEED has a multistakeholder base of support, is committed to ongoing improvement, and is currently the most widely used rating system in the United States.

The LEED system was developed and is administered by the United States Green Building Council (USGBC, www.usgbc.org), a voluntary, committee-based, nongovernmental organization initiated in 1993. The USGBC is a consortium of building owners, suppliers, contractors, architects, engineers, governmental agencies, and others involved in the building process. A nonprofit organization with nearly sixteen thousand member companies,[8] the consortium's primary goal is to develop an approach to building design that is healthy, profitable, and environmentally sustainable. By the late 1990s, the USGBC began testing LEED, a rating system that provides guidance in making choices consistent with the goals of creation care and is designed to be open to continual scrutiny and revision.

The LEED rating system has become an industry standard for green building in the United States and around the world (LEED projects are currently found in all fifty states and 106 countries). The initial rating system was developed for new construction. Through the years the system has expanded and now addresses multiple building applications, including schools, health care, and homes, as well as new construction (LEED-NC), existing buildings (LEED-EB), commercial interiors (LEED-CI), core and shell construction (LEED-CS), and neighborhood development (LEED-ND), a rating system developed in collaboration with Congress for the New Urbanism and the Natural Resources Defense Council. Rating systems for guiding retail building are also available. Version 1.0 of LEED was released in August 1998. The current version of 3.0 was released in April 2009 (LEED 2009). The first religious congregational project was certified in 2005. As of July 2011 eighteen faith communities (two Jewish and sixteen Christian) had received LEED certification and sixty projects were registered to seek certification.[9] A database for searching LEED-certified projects is available via the USGBC website.

Congregations that want to take a comprehensive approach to creation care through green building can apply for recognition of a new construction or major renovation project or for an existing building. Four levels of recognition are possible: certified (minimum level), silver, gold, and platinum (maximum level). Six areas are considered in the new-construction and existing-building checklists: sustainability of the site, water efficiency, energy and atmosphere, materials and resources, indoor environmental quality, and innovation in design (for LEED-NC) or innovation in operations (for LEED-EB).

> *Sustainability of the site* includes site selection, community connectivity (integration into the neighborhood with emphasis on enhancing pedestrian access), transportation (including public transportation and alternative forms of transportation), storm-water management (rainwater runoff), protection and conservation of the building site (minimal disturbance and leaving open space), generation of heat (minimizing radiant heat via paved areas and roofs), and light pollution (excess light at night).

Water efficiency includes plumbing efficiency, landscaping measures, and wastewater management.

Energy and atmosphere includes energy optimization, refrigerant management, and on-site renewable energy production (including solar, wind, and biomass).

Materials and resources includes storing and collecting recyclables, existing building and existing materials reuse, construction waste management, and use of materials derived from recycled content or renewable materials and available regionally.

Indoor environmental quality includes air delivery and ventilation, use of low-emitting materials (for adhesives, sealants, paints, coatings, flooring, and furnishings), lighting and comfort system controllability, and attention to daylighting.

Innovation in design (for LEED-NC) or *innovation in operations* (for LEED-EB) includes unique environmental stewardship efforts (for example, community presentations featuring the green building practices of the project) and use of a LEED-accredited professional.

Regional priority credits can also be earned for addressing geographically specific environmental priorities (predetermined to be especially important for each location). Documentation is required to substantiate achievements in each area on the checklist and is primarily done online. Designating someone to oversee the certification process is essential to successfully implementing LEED.

The USGBC holds regular workshops for those interested in learning more about green building design. Training for professionals who would like to work as consultants for helping clients achieve a LEED rating is also offered. In 2011 more than 162,000 LEED Green Associates and LEED Accredited Professionals (LEED AP) were registered with the USGBC (including many architects). Congregations would be best served by working with an accredited professional throughout the entire building project, should they desire to pursue LEED recognition.

Costs associated with participation in the LEED program include membership in the USGBC (varies depending on the organizational category and gross annual revenue; recommended for the price discount on services realized by members, but not required), a registration fee when the project begins, a fee to cover certification expenses (based on square footage of the project), and labor needed to oversee, document, and submit the needed data. Current USGBC dues and fees can be found through their website. Here are some examples of costs for using LEED 2009 from mid-2011:

- A faith community could join under the nonprofit category for $300 (as a 501(c)(3) with a budget less than $15 million).
- Project registration would be $900 for a member or $1,200 for a nonmember. (Neighborhood-wide development and multiple building projects will vary.)
- Certification fees for a new construction project, combined design and construction review, of less than 50,000 square feet would be $2,250 for a member or $2,750 for a nonmember. For an existing building project, initial certification review of less than 50,000 square feet it would be $1,500 for a member or $2,000 for a nonmember.

Membership in the USGBC will more than pay for itself in savings on fees, access to additional materials, and discounts on supporting resources. The combined design and construction review allows planners to make clarifications or slight adjustments prior to final submission of a project for certification. Costs are minimized when LEED goals guide the design and construction of a project from the very beginning. It is important that all parties connected to the project adhere to the sustainable goals and follow through on implementing the intended design.

Questions have been raised through the years about the cost of implementing the LEED certification process. The USGBC website has a Green Building Research page that links" to "Research Publications," which includes a section on "Cost Analysis of Whole Buildings."[10] More than a dozen articles discuss LEED-oriented and non-LEED-oriented cost-benefit analyses.[11] Among the LEED-oriented studies there is a general consensus that achieving the equivalent of a LEED silver design adds 1 to 2 percent on average in construction costs to a project (although many projects realized no additional expenses over conventional construction).[12] When approached with intention from the beginning, green building strategies are not an add-on expense but a more holistic, integrated, and environmentally responsible way to design. When requirements for achieving higher levels of LEED recognition are sought, additional construction expenses can add up to 8 percent to construction costs, depending on a host of issues (for example, building type, location, and features desired).

Costs associated with LEED can be recovered through decreases in operating costs and higher building value. According to data from the USGBC, green buildings can reduce energy use by 24 to 50 percent, carbon dioxide emissions by 33 to 39 percent, water use by 40 percent, and solid waste by 70 percent. Perceived business benefits to building green include an 8 to 9 percent decrease in operating costs, a 7.5 percent increase in building value, a 3.5 percent increase in occupancy ratio, a 3 percent increase in rent ratio, and a 6.6 percent improvement in return on investment.[13] The economic benefits that emerge from green building demonstrate this approach to be wise financial and environmental stewardship.

It is important to note that LEED certification is only one tool to help congregations model and achieve creation care. A congregation can pursue green building without engaging in the LEED certification process. The various levels of certification can be achieved without LEED verification. And the actual building may not perform as projected even when using LEED. The potential, powerful benefits of LEED certification need to be carefully considered. Pursuing LEED certification can help a community learn more about ways stewardship of the environment can be achieved through the property a congregation is entrusted to manage. LEED can function as a helpful accountability partner in fulfilling green building intentions. And LEED-certified buildings can become effective tools for sharing ways of sustainable living with others. Positive relationships can be built among faith communities and between a faith community and its surrounding community. The potential creation-care benefits of even a certified LEED project are contingent on a commitment from the congregation to monitor and maintain the ecofriendly strategies incorporated into the building. Ongoing effort is needed for the congregation to maximize the creation-care potential of its facilities. One generation will need to teach the next the importance of green building, and all will need to share in the work of maintaining a sustainable lifestyle.

HISTORIC BUILDINGS:
SUSTAINABLE PRESERVATION AND ADAPTIVE USE

Sometimes we tend to think of only new construction or renovation projects as candidates for embracing green building goals. When we think in this way, we miss the inherent green benefits of historic preservation. People in the United States have sought to conserve the built environment since the early part of the nineteenth century, even before the movement to conserve the natural environment. As our country developed, people recognized the aesthetic beauty, unique architectural features, fine craftsmanship and materials, historical significance, and deep meanings, generated especially in local communities, of buildings from earlier decades. The designation "historic" has developed over time and is applied to buildings and properties that have been recognized by oversight agencies as architecturally or historically significant enough to preserve and maintain. Buildings and properties must be evaluated to determine if they qualify for this distinctive recognition and its tangible benefits. Preserving historic buildings and properties—retaining existing assets and renewing or retooling them—for their original or new uses is an important form of creation care. Land, raw materials, and energy can be conserved through preservation and reuse efforts, often incorporating green building practices.

National and state agencies have been established through the years to organize and promote historic preservation initiatives. The National Trust for Historic Preservation (NTHP, www.preservationnation.org) was established in 1949 under the leadership of President Harry Truman to identify and preserve important buildings of many types throughout the country. The National Historic Preservation Act was passed in 1966, establishing the National Register of Historic Places (www.nps.gov/nr), which is administered by the National Park Service. More than eighty thousand properties are officially recognized on this registry today, including many synagogues and churches. To qualify for financial assistance to offset expenses related to preserving the building and its property, the owner of the historic property must register the site.

The State Historic Preservation Officers (local office websites available at www.nps.gov/nr/shpolist.htm) were also established through the National Historic Preservation Act. The state office cooperates with national, state, and local governmental agencies and the private sector to assist historic preservation activities. Resources for achieving national registry and preservation work are available in each state through this network of offices. Matching grants to support local historic preservation projects began to be awarded through the Preservation Services Fund in 1969.

In 1998 the National Trust for Historic Preservation became a privately funded agency. In 2001 Touro Synagogue, Newport, Rhode Island, completed in 1763 and restored for the first time in 1828,[14] became the first faith community property named a National Trust Historic Site. Twenty-nine sites (two of which are religious buildings) are maintained by the NTHP at this time. Numerous Christian and Jewish properties not designated as NTHP sites are also featured via the NTHP website to recognize their outstanding preservation work. A sampling of historic synagogues and churches includes Lloyd Street Synagogue (1845), Baltimore, Maryland; Metropolitan AME Church (1886), Washington, DC; St. Paul's Episcopal Church (1899), Hamilton, Montana; Holy Trinity Russian Orthodox Cathedral (1903), Chicago, Illinois; Unity Temple (1906–09), Oak Park, Illinois;

and Beth Sholom Synagogue (1959), Elkins Park, Pennsylvania. In 1988 the NTHP initiated an annual list of buildings and properties entitled "America's 11 Most Endangered Historic Places" to mobilize concern and resources for preservation efforts on a national scale. Recent lists have included Unity Temple (in 2009) and Metropolitan AME, Washington, DC (in 2010).

Including churches and synagogues in networks of historic preservation activities on national and state levels demonstrates the value our society places on religious historic buildings and properties. Congregations need not pursue historic preservation and adaptive use in isolation. We have resources of many kinds that will help us achieve our goals of creation care through preservation activities. The national and state agencies noted above provide a multitude of documents and initiatives to help owners of properties consider and pursue historic preservation efforts. An agency that exists particularly for faith communities seeking to invest in their older properties is Partners for Sacred Places (www.sacredplaces.org). The organization offers training, workshops, conferences, and publications to congregations. Partners for Sacred Places can also assist with developing initiatives to encourage new resources for older religious properties. A downloadable, free document, "Sacred Places at Risk: New Evidence on How Endangered Older Churches and Synagogues Serve Communities," explains the significance of social services and community activities achieved through older religious communities and their buildings. Direct ministries and sharing our buildings with members and nonmembers alike constitutes a sizeable presence in our cities for promoting the common good. A strong case is made in this document for remaining in existing facilities. Upward of ten thousand print and multimedia resources related to fund-raising, building maintenance, sharing space, and serving families are available through the website. Material accessed via the "Building Maintenance" link under "Information Center" includes guidance for pursuing environmental stewardship in the preservation process.

Historic preservation includes a range of activities that the United States Department of the Interior describes in "Standards for Preservation and Guidelines for Preserving Historic Buildings" (www.nps.gov/history/hps/tps/standguide/). Preserving, rehabilitating, restoring, and reconstructing are four primary treatments that can be pursued for historic buildings. The treatments are briefly defined in the overview to the guide as follows:

> The first treatment, **Preservation**, places a high premium on the retention of all historic fabric through conservation, maintenance and repair. It reflects a building's continuum over time, through successive occupancies, and the respectful changes and alterations that are made.
>
> **Rehabilitation**, the second treatment, emphasizes the retention and repair of historic materials, but more latitude is provided for replacement because it is assumed the property is more deteriorated prior to work. (Both Preservation and Rehabilitation standards focus attention on the preservation of those materials, features, finishes, spaces, and spatial relationships that, together, give a property its historic character.)
>
> **Restoration**, the third treatment, focuses on the retention of materials from the most significant time in a property's history, while permitting the removal of materials from other periods.
>
> **Reconstruction**, the fourth treatment, establishes limited opportunities to re-create a non-surviving site, landscape, building, structure, or object in all new materials.[15]

More detailed definitions, standards, and guidelines for each treatment can be found in the document. Sections of the guide address exterior materials, exterior features, interior features, the site, the setting, and special requirements for each treatment. The standards and guidelines are not prescriptive but establish a base from which congregations can make consistent choices in the preservation process.

Fundamentally, historic preservation, treasuring and maintaining the resources that have been inherited from earlier generations, is an act of creation care. Preservation involves less dramatic development, lower natural material use, and less waste. The National

Trust for Historic Preservation focuses a portion of its website on sustainability. The site notes the synergistic relationship that can be established between historic preservation and sustainable choices, and it includes green tips for individuals and communities, relevant news items, information on their preservation green lab, and case studies of buildings that achieved sustainable historic preservation. It reports that the Leadership in Energy and Environmental Design (LEED) rating system has been applied to historic preservation projects in recent years. More than thirty historic buildings across the country have been LEED certified to date. If a congregation would like to pursue historic preservation in light of sustainable design principles, it would be important to select professionals knowledgeable in these areas to provide the appropriate guidance.

Trinity Church (1876), Boston, Massachusetts, is an example of a historic church preservation project concerned about reflecting creation care. Featured on the sustainability page of the National Trust for Historic Preservation website, the church, which maintained major elements of the existing structure, incorporated the following features:

- 12,000 square feet of new, occupiable space within existing naturally insulated foundation walls
- 100 percent storm-water management (managing rainfall with maximum effectiveness)
- New geothermal ground-source heat pump system for heating and cooling (six wells driven 1,500 feet into the ground next to the building)
- Operable windows for natural ventilation in new meeting spaces
- Carbon dioxide sensors to maximize fresh air ventilation
- Water-saving plumbing fixtures in new and existing restrooms
- Energy-saving light fixtures with sensors for occupancy and settings for flexible light levels

- Use of recycled content materials and local and re-gional materials, including reuse of salvaged material
- Use of low VOC-compliant materials for all paint, carpet, adhesives, and composite wood[16]

Many features of the church, such as its stained glass, decorative paint, sandstone statuary and details, tile and slate roofs, and interior furniture were addressed in the project. Health and safety dimensions of the building were brought up to code. The firm in charge of the restoration project, Goody Clancy, integrated green design features into each phase of the overall project.

With thoughtful planning, the natural features of older buildings can contribute in substantial ways to green building. Many older buildings were designed to minimize energy consumption and maximize daylight and natural ventilation through passive systems simply as a matter of course. Building orientation, use of durable materials, room dimensions, and the ratio of windows to wall surface area are examples of such features. Green building today is looking back to earlier models of building to recover these sometimes neglected dimensions of design. Two projects that are combining historic preservation with creation care will be featured later in this book: Eldridge Street Synagogue (1887), New York City, through the work of the Museum at Eldridge Street, and Unity Temple (1906–09), Oak Park, Illinois, through the work of the Unity Temple Restoration Foundation. Dimensions of each project will be noted in several of the next chapters to further illustrate ways to achieve sustainable preservation work.

CONCLUSIONS

Green building is an effective strategy for new construction, renovation, or historic preservation projects to achieve active creation care. Green building is as ancient as humanity. For faith communities that acknowledge their biblical mandate to be good stewards of the gift of the natural world, green building is a timely opportunity to exercise environmental, economic, and social responsibility. Increasing the performance of our buildings is a helpful first step, but we will need to pursue holistic changes in our life choices to achieve restorative and regenerative levels of green building that are truly sustainable. Many tools exist that could help congregations navigate the emerging world of green building. Certification programs, Energy Star, and the LEED rating system can all contribute to our understanding of the sustainable qualities of various products and how they best work together to minimize or eliminate our carbon footprint, provide maximum benefits for healthy living, and work toward healing the earth. Green building is not an expensive add-on feature but an essential guiding principle comparable to conventional building costs and yields economic benefits throughout the life cycle of the building. With a commitment to green building goals, any style of building from any time period can be an avenue through which a faith community can pursue creation care.

CHAPTER 4

Models for Creation Care Building and Renovation

Congregations throughout the United States and Canada have been involved in creation care through their property and buildings in increasing numbers over the past twenty years. Reasons for these initiatives have included an acknowledgment of a biblical mandate for stewardship of the earth, a recognition of unsustainable patterns of living, financial incentives for going green, and a desire to provide leadership for environmental responsibility in one's neighborhood. A renewed appreciation for the beauty and wonder of the natural world often follows in the wake of creation care. Ten congregations that have participated in varying levels of creation care in and through their communal setting will be featured in this chapter. The congregations are located in Arkansas, California, Illinois, Maryland, Michigan, New York, Wisconsin, and Ontario, Canada. The congregations are located in urban, suburban, and rural settings. Some are larger and some are smaller. Economic resources vary, as do the levels of green building achieved to this point. Each setting suggests a range of potential sustainable activities.

Among them, the ten congregations carried out five new construction buildings, three renovation or expansion projects, and two historic preservation projects. Six of the projects received Leadership in Energy and Environmental Design (LEED) recognition for their work. Two are the first platinum-level LEED certified projects in the category of religious buildings. These congregations illustrate a host of sustainable building options, and I hope they will inspire other communities to move from intention to action.

NEW CONSTRUCTION PROJECTS

KEYSTONE COMMUNITY CHURCH (SPAULDING CAMPUS)
ADA, MICHIGAN
www.keystonecc.org

Keystone Community Church began as a new church plant under the direction of Pastor Gene DeJong in 1997. The congregation of 1,300 people is active on two campuses. The larger campus is featured here. Although its original affiliation was with the Christian Reformed Church, Keystone is now an independent, nondenominational community of faith. When the congregation began to think about building its first permanent place for worship and ministry, leaders included creation care as a part of the vision. Taking responsibility for stewardship of the earth's resources was a primary impetus for examining green design alternatives. Pastor DeJong sought a way to help his faith community translate good intentions concerning stewardship of the earth into concrete action. The fact that green building could yield financial savings in relation to energy costs and support businesses in the local area were additional dimensions of stewardship that appealed to the community.

Keystone purchased a thirty-five acre site in Ada, a small township adjacent to Grand Rapids, Michigan. The site had rolling hills, heavy woods, and wetlands. High priorities were to preserve the beauty of this natural setting and to inspire the congregation. Integrated Architecture, Grand Rapids, was selected to design the new church. Integrated Architecture had extensive experience with designing sustainable buildings, although the firm had never been asked to design a religious building prior to this project. The firm's architects introduced the church leadership to LEED, and the church made certification a goal from the beginning of the project. This decision influenced numerous decisions throughout the design and building process and helped to keep creation care a top priority. Rockford Construction Company, Grand Rapids, served as the general contractor for the project.

The church building has two levels that yield 33,000 square feet of space, including a five-hundred-seat auditorium, classrooms, youth areas, a prayer room, church offices, and a café-like central gathering area. The overall cost for the project was approximately $3 million. The building was completed in August 2004 and was awarded LEED certification in 2005. Keystone was the first Christian community to receive LEED certification for a worship space in the United States. Integrated Architecture earned an Honor Award in 2006 from the American Institute of Architects in Michigan in recognition of the excellence of Keystone's sustainable design.

Keystone used a contemporary design in building their church. They place a high priority on reaching out to people who have never been part of a congregation or those who have been disenfranchised from church life, so leaders wanted to minimize traditional symbolism associated with church architecture. They were careful in the placement of their building on their site, the design of the building, and the materials used in construction. More details about specific aspects of the building will be incorporated into the next three chapters to help illustrate the creation care potential of religious buildings.

The choice to pursue creation care through land development and building construction is supplemented by green choices in congregational life. Visitors who encounter Keystone are greeted with a new, reusable shopping bag that contains information and gifts from the church. One piece of literature, "In L.E.E.D. and Green at Keystone!" explains the ways in which creation care is manifest in and through the work of the community. An extensive recycling program is ongoing through the church, with recycling stations for a variety of materials located inside and outside the building. (Directions and lists of recyclable materials are distributed to regular attenders and visitors.) Mugs and glasses used in the café are washed and reused. Sermons occasionally address environmental stewardship and challenge the congregation to act as responsible stewards of the creation. Creation care is emphasized as an ongoing expression of the life of faith, corporately and individually, through these efforts.

St. Gabriel of the Sorrowful Virgin Church
Toronto, Ontario, Canada
www.stgabrielsparish.ca

St. Gabriel of the Sorrowful Virgin Church is located in North York, an ethnically diverse community of three thousand parishioners in northern Toronto. St. Gabriel's is a Catholic faith community established by the Passionist order. Father Paul J. Cusack is the current senior pastor. The Passionists were founded in Italy in 1747 by St. Paul of the Cross as an order of itinerant preachers who focused on proclaiming the passion, death, and resurrection of Jesus Christ. The parish was established in North York in 1951 and built its first modern-style brick structure in 1953 as part of a Passionist Canadian seminary. Over time the congregation outgrew its building, and the Passionist community and parishioners of St. Gabriel's decided in 1998 to build a new church. Creation care became an important dimension of the project. Originally St. Gabriel's owned three hectares (nearly seven and one-half acres) of land. Much of the property was sold to assist with fund-raising for the new church building. They currently occupy just under one hectare (two acres).

St. Gabriel Church drew inspiration for stewardship of the earth from the writings of Thomas Berry (1914–2009), a priest and theologian in the Passionist order. Berry articulated a tremendous concern for establishing a mutually beneficial relationship between humanity and the earth. He deeply appreciated the spiritual dimension of earth care. St. Gabriel's wanted to emphasize the connection between the sacredness of the faith community and the sacredness of the creation in its new building. Excerpts from Berry's writings appear on a series of markers distributed throughout the garden on the south side of the building to remind people of the intimate connection between humanity and the creation.

Roberto Chiotti, a founding partner of Larkin Architect Limited in Toronto, was chosen to lead the design for St. Gabriel's new church building project. Chiotti, in addition to being an accredited LEED architect, attained a master's degree in theological studies with a focus in theology and ecology. Chiotti drew inspiration from Berry's reflections in conceiving of the design for St. Gabriel's.[1] The entire building process, from design to construction and furnishing, incorporated choices meant to enhance the relationship between humanity and the creation. The building stands two stories high. It covers approximately 21,500 square feet. The interior includes a 750-seat sanctuary for worship, with a reservation chapel and a reconciliation room; spacious narthex; offices; meeting rooms; and other support facilities. Construction of the church began in March 2005 and continued to July 2006. St. Gabriel Church received LEED certification at the gold level for its building, the first church in Canada to receive this recognition. In 2007 the church received the Green Toronto Award for outstanding green building design. The overall cost of the project, including underground parking for 113 automobiles, was approximately $10.5 million.

The building exhibits a contemporary design. The walls are poured-in-place concrete, with concrete used for the ceiling and floors as well. A unique limestone from the province of Manitoba was used on the exterior surface of the narthex. The limestone contains many embedded fossils of ancient sea creatures, a reference to the geological history of the area and connection to the natural world. The worship space and liturgical appointments are oriented on a north-south axis. On the north end, near the reservation chapel, is the altar. At the south end of the space is the ambo and baptismal font. The font is next to a glass curtain wall that constitutes the southern façade. Rows of pews, reclaimed from the original church and refurbished, are arranged on either side of the rectangular central space containing the liturgical appointments, which is an antiphonal arrangement where the seating is split on either side of a central space. The presider's chair is located at the center bank of pews, terminating the entrance axis. The entrance is on the long, east side of the space. The glass-curtain wall, set at a five-degree angle to help with glare reduction, provides much natural light and grants an excellent view of the garden. A large cantilevered canopy extends over the southern façade to assist with harvesting the winter sun's energy and shading the building in the summer. Skylights are located around the perimeter of the worship space for additional natural light. Stained glass is incorporated into the skylight, along with dichroic glass panels, to add a dimension of color to the light. Dichroic glass contains microthin layers of metals, metal oxides, or silica that refract light into different colors depending on the angle of the source. The two types of glass provide washes of color across the interior concrete surfaces as the sun moves across the sky, varying according to weather conditions and season of the year. Yellow tones emphasize the light of the sun on the south end of the space, with azure blue and crimson tones produced toward the north end. The use of color adds to the symbolism of journey from the baptismal font to the altar and tabernacle.

The features of the new green design are shared via the church website. Under the tab "Who We Are" on the homepage is the link "Green Church." The section includes reflections on the theological significance of the sustainable church design, written by the architect, and details about the engineering of the building. These pages inform and remind the congregation and visitors of the meaning and value of having a green building for worship and ministry.

An interactive computer kiosk in the narthex highlights the ecotheology and LEED initiatives of the building. Discrete signage describes the various green strategies pursued as they relate to creation care. Worship activities include a monthly Sunday celebration that highlights ecological themes reflected in the week's Scripture readings and special solstice services. Educational activities include classes on the teachings of Thomas Berry and ongoing building tours and lectures. All maintenance procedures, including groundskeeping, comprehensive recycling, and cleaning and cleaning supplies, are ecofriendly. And green energy use is promoted through purchasing carbon neutral electricity from the local utility.

CONGREGATION BETH DAVID
SAN LUIS OBISPO, CALIFORNIA
www.cbdslo.org

Congregation Beth David was founded in 1959 and is a member of the Union for Reform Judaism.[2] Its congregation has roots in French and German immigrant groups who became established in San Luis Obispo in the mid-nineteenth century. Rabbi Scott Corngold is the current leader of this faith community consisting of approximately 180 families. An initial synagogue building was constructed in 1960 for the congregation. By 1975 the community had outgrown the facilities, and a process of planning for expansion and seeking new property ensued. Paul Wolff, a member of the congregation and professor of architecture at California Polytechnic State University, San Luis Obispo, assisted the community in exploring a variety of models for potential synagogue designs. In 2001 Congregation Beth David purchased ninety-two acres of land on the edge of the city, an act that brought a twenty-five-year search to a conclusion.

The congregation made a commitment to pursue a green building project on its new property. Members engaged the architectural services of San Luis Sustainability Group (SLSG), Santa Margarita, California, under the principal leadership of Polly Cooper and Ken Haggard. SLSG specializes in green architecture and sustainable planning. They have been developing environmentally conscious residential and commercial projects since 1976. Haggard and Cooper have written, published, and presented papers on passive solar building,[3] straw bale building, natural air conditioning, and sustainable fractal architecture design.[4] Passive solar heating, solar energy production, natural ventilation, sustainable building methods, and straw bale construction were all incorporated into Congregation Beth David's new synagogue. S. J. Deferville Construction was selected as the general contractor for the project and worked closely with the congregation and the architects during the design phase.

Construction of Congregation Beth David's building began in June 2005 and was completed in December 2006. A vernacular style of design was used for the synagogue, inspired by farm complexes with windrows. It is designed in the general shape of a bagel, with the building oriented around a central courtyard. The entrance includes a trellis, the design of which echoes the sanctuary roof. The crossbeams of the trellis form a stylized version of the Hebrew priestly benediction gesture—two hands with thumbs touching held up toward the congregation. The building includes a sanctuary facing east, which is traditional for synagogues; chapel social hall; lobby; library; conference room; classrooms; full kitchen; youth lounge; gift shop; and administrative offices. The sanctuary seats 337, but the capacity can be expanded to 460 with removable soundproof partitions. The building is 16,190 square feet in size. Artificial lighting is not ordinarily needed in the building during daylight hours. Achieving LEED accreditation was a goal from the beginning of the project. When the congregation began its project, no synagogue had yet been LEED certified. Seeking LEED certification set the tone for the entire project. Volunteers from within the congregation generated the documentation necessary to apply for LEED recognition. Basic LEED certification was awarded in 2007, making the building the first synagogue in the world to attain this distinction.

Thirteen of the ninety-two acres were developed for the synagogue building and for parking. Sixty-two acres were reserved for agriculture and permanent open space. The overall project cost approximately $6.3 million (1 million for the land, plus 1.2 million for architecture, permits, studies, and other soft costs, plus 1.6 million for site development, plus 2.5 million for the building or $156 per square foot). Construction was completed within half a percent of the budget. Energy costs in the first two years of occupancy were 38 percent below the California Title 24 standard (energy efficiency standards for residential and nonresidential buildings). The congregation saves 108,000 kilowatts per hour of electricity annually over standard designs, which represents a savings of fifty-nine tons of CO_2 (carbon dioxide emissions).

A Green Shalom program for the congregation emerged following construction of the new building. The intention was to assist the people in pursuing a sustainable lifestyle in concert with the
principles that guided the building design. Monthly programs have
been offered for education and fulfilling creation care. Program
topics have addressed fair trade food, recycling, green gardening,
shopping with a conscience (avoiding sweatshop products), green
cleaning supplies, socially responsible investing, and compact fluorescent lighting. The congregation has also joined together with
the local ministerial association to pursue community-wide creation care. The website of the congregation features reflections on
the green design of the synagogue. On the homepage, under the
tab "About Us," is a link to "Our Green Synagogue." The green
synagogue web page includes a general description of the site and
exterior and interior of the building. A section entitled "Tikkun
Olam" details various ways in which the site and building ex-
emplify creation care. The congregation has developed multiple
documents recalling and celebrating the design and construction
of the synagogue as well. Circulation of these materials reminds
the congregation of the reasons behind its sustainable intentions
and shares these insights with those who are new to the community. Creation care is a way of life that requires remembering and
reaffirmation.

Jewish Reconstructionist Congregation
Evanston, Illinois
www.jrc-evanston.org

Jewish Reconstructionist Congregation (JRC) is a member of the
Jewish Reconstructionist Federation.[5] Reconstructionism is an
American movement within Judaism, founded in 1922 on principles established by Rabbi Mordecai M. Kaplan. Rabbi Brant
Rosen, leader of JRC, has been active in social justice activities for
decades and helped to focus his community's commitment to fulfilling creation care through the design of a new synagogue. Green
building was a new concept to many within his congregation, so
Rabbi Rosen allowed for a process of conversation and discov-
ery in developing congregational commitment to the project. He

sought to involve his congregation in learning about sustainable building and applying its principles to its particular context rather than simply insist on sustainable ideas for a potential building project. JRC recognized that erecting a sustainable religious building is only the first step in establishing a sustainable lifestyle. Daily choices must be made in congregational life to maintain the potential of green building.

In May 2003 JRC made a commitment to pursue the highest LEED certification attainable within the limitations of the project (a gold or platinum level). JRC chose Carol Ross Barney and Michael A. Ross of Ross Barney Architects, Chicago, to design the new building. Bulley and Andrews, LLC, Chicago, was selected to be the general contractor for the project. Analysis of the congregation's building program revealed that using some spaces for multiple purposes, creating flexible space, would reduce the space needed by over 10,000 square feet, compared with a design in which each room was dedicated to a single purpose. Groundbreaking occurred in October 2006, and the first service was celebrated in February 2008.

A three-story building of 31,600 square feet (33 percent larger that the original building) was built on the site of the previous synagogue. The primary portal is made of white limestone tiles imported from Israel, Jerusalem stone (creating a historical link to this religiously important location), along with a two-story ceremonial wood door made of maple harvested from the site—a dramatic entry point. Administrative offices, a small sanctuary, gift shop, and early childhood center are located on the first floor. Religious school classrooms and offices, a youth lounge, and library are located on the second floor. The main sanctuary, social hall, and kitchen are on the third floor. A moveable divider between the main sanctuary and social hall allows for flexible use of the space, ranging from worship seating for a maximum of 500 people to a sit-down dinner for 250. The unique divider is a bifold aluminum aircraft hangar door that folds up to the ceiling. LEED goals were integrated into each dimension of the design and building process.

In the fall of 2008 JRC was awarded LEED platinum certification and became the first religious building in the United States to attain the highest certification possible. In the spring of 2009 the

American Institute of Architects Committee on the Environment selected JRC's new synagogue to be one of its Top Ten Green Projects for the year. The overall cost of the project was approximately $10 million (construction costs were about 7.3 million of this total). Costs associated with achieving this LEED platinum-certified green building were about 7.5 percent of the overall project cost. JRC chose not to incorporate every sustainable option available. They decided not to incorporate a green roof, geothermal heating or cooling, and permeable pavement in the parking area. Each community needs to consider the large array of options available today and then make the best choices possible given the limitations of the congregation.

In an effort to help guide sustainable daily choices in congregational life, JRC generated a green policy statement and guidelines for implementation. Ideally, the guidelines move from implementation in the congregation to life outside the congregation as well. A general policy statement was posted in January 2008 on the website to share the vision the congregation has for fulfilling creation care in daily practice. The policy includes commitments to reduce the use of depletable energy resources, increase use of recycled and recyclable materials, reduce contributions to landfills, purchase products and services in light of sustainable ideals, conserve water, reduce the community's use of toxic substances, increase use of biodegradable cleaning products, reduce emissions of greenhouse gases, and conduct ongoing audits and reviews to track annual compliance. Celebrations of many kinds are held in the synagogue throughout the year. In an effort to apply sustainable principles to celebrations, the congregation developed a "Preferred Simcha Plan." It gives practical suggestions for how to implement green choices in relation to invitations, religious service guides, room and table decorations, food and food service, waste management, give-away gifts, and transportation.

A "Green Procedures Manual and Plan for Environmentally Preferable Purchasing" was also developed. Energy efficiency, waste from paper and office, food and food service procedures, transportation, waste disposal, cleaning and maintenance supplies and services, and landscaping are all addressed in detail. JRC is pursuing green building with a restorative and regenerative end

in mind. The original goals of creation care are continually rein-
forced through this intentional effort to alter consumption and
waste patterns. Creation care is not something that fades into the
background life of the community, as if it had been completed
through building a LEED platinum synagogue.

The home page of the JRC website provides the tab "Green
Synagogue," with links to five articles. "Judaism and the
Environment" outlines the impact that buildings have in general
on our environment (energy use, greenhouse gas emissions, raw
materials use, waste output, and potable water consumption).
Environmental, economic, health, and community benefits associated with sustainable buildings are noted as well. Details about the
green building project are found under "Our Building." The link
also includes a virtual tour of the building, awards the building
has received, and the LEED certification announcement. Docent-
led tours of the synagogue can be scheduled via the website.
Frequently asked questions are addressed under "Ask Us," including a brief explanation of LEED and a method to ask further questions. And under "Resources" links can be found to the documents
noted above: "Greening Your Simcha," "Green Building Policies,"
and "Green Procedures Manual and Plan for Environmentally
Preferable Purchasing." Local recycling programs for chemicals,
electronics, and clothing are also included. JRC has created an
effective avenue for sharing materials to assist their congregation,
as well as those beyond their congregation, to pursue sustainable
living.

HOLY WISDOM MONASTERY
MIDDLETON, WISCONSIN
www.benedictinewomen.org

The Benedictine Women of Madison, an organization of Christian
sisters who moved from Iowa to the Madison Diocese in 1953,
established Holy Wisdom Monastery. In the mid-1960s the
Benedictine sisters opened Saint Benedict Center, a retreat and
conference facility for Christians and seekers of all world reli-
gions. Prayer, hospitality, justice, and creation care are central to
the mission of the community. In 1998 the monastic community

opened its membership to women of all Christian traditions, while remaining in federation with other Benedictine sisters. Varying levels of affiliation exist in the community, such that some members are full-time residents at Holy Wisdom Monastery and others (oblates) participate regularly in retreats while maintaining residence in other locations. Sister Mary David Walgenbach is the prioress of the community.

Holy Wisdom Monastery is located on a 138-acre parcel of farmland just west of Madison, Wisconsin. In 1953 the Sisters purchased an initial forty-two acres, and additional acreage was purchased from 1960 to the 1990s. A girls' high school was begun in 1958, and by 1966 the high school was closed. The main school building, which was 60,000 square feet, was renovated by the sisters into Benedict House, the primary retreat and conference building of the community. Opportunities to care for the land were pursued by the sisters in the decades that followed. (More about this will be said in chapter 5.)

In the mid-1990s the community recognized that Saint Benedict Center needed some significant renovation work. Evaluation of the Benedict House building yielded estimates in the neighborhood of $5 million for a complete renovation. The high costs associated with maintaining this large, older building suggested replacing it. A plan to build a smaller facility that exemplified environmental stewardship was developed, with an ultimate goal of achieving a zero carbon footprint. The new building was erected on the site of the old one. Construction of the new building began in June 2008, and the building was completed in July 2009.

The Benedictine Women of Madison contracted with Hoffman LLC, Appleton, Wisconsin, for the project. The new two-story building is approximately 34,000 square feet. It includes areas for gathering, worship, dining, meeting, offices, and a library. A decision was made by the sisters to pursue LEED accreditation on this project at the platinum level. About $150,000 was needed to fulfill the LEED process. Holy Wisdom Monastery became the first Christian community to receive LEED recognition at the platinum level in the spring of 2010. It was awarded sixty-three out of a possible sixty-nine points, the highest number of points awarded to any project at that time. Overall, the cost of the new building was just under $8 million, including decommissioning Benedict House and all furnishings. The new building is a model for green design and sustainable living. By July 2010, more than two thousand visitors had toured the facilities, including groups of students from nearby schools, colleges, and universities. A significant role in creation care is being modeled via the land restoration and green building design of the community.

Holy Wisdom Monastery shares its creation care approach and achievements in multiple ways on its website. "Care for the Earth" provides information about volunteering to care for the land of the community, seasonal nature notes, a brief history of the sisters' environmental work, educational opportunities available through the resources of the monastery, and suggestions for sustainable living. A trail map and guide to the grounds has been developed for visitors. Four trails ranging from 0.3 to 2.0 miles in length have been created to allow the surrounding community to enjoy the flora and fauna of the setting. Indeed, the trails provide an excellent landscape to accompany the many retreats that Holy Wisdom Monastery facilitates. Funding of the environmental restoration and preservation efforts of the sisters is underwritten in part through its "AcreMaker Club." Donations via this club have supported a summer college internship program, a naturalist and restoration ecologist who works with the monastery, and environmental volunteer programs.

RENOVATION AND EXPANSION PROJECTS

TEMPLE EMANUEL
KENSINGTON, MARYLAND
www.templeemanuelmd.org

Temple Emanuel, a community of about five hundred families, was organized in 1952 and affiliated with the Union of American Hebrew Congregations (now, Union for Reform Judaism) in 1953. A building for the congregation was completed by 1958 on its five-acre site. Expansions and renovations to the building occurred in 1974 and 2002. Rabbi Warren Stone, the present leader of the community, has been active in environmental concerns for more than thirty years. In 1993 he became a founding board member of the Coalition on the Environment and Jewish Life (COEJL), and he was a writer and contributor to the *Green Faith Guide* (2004) developed by the Washington, DC, Energy Office (the interreligious environmental action manual mentioned in chapter 2). He has also been active in attending both the 1997 Kyoto and the 2009 Copenhagen international climate talks.

Rabbi Stone facilitated the establishment of a Green Shalom Committee at Temple Emanuel in 1989–90 shortly after beginning his ministry in the community. In 1992 the Green Shalom Committee proposed an environmental policy for Temple Emanuel. The policy, updated in December 2003, includes the following goals: schedule an audit by PEPCO (a regional energy provider) of the temple's new facilities and seek regular audits; develop and implement a comprehensive landscaping plan; complete and maintain a small, biblically inspired garden; work with local environmental organizations (such as the Kensington Ministerium, Shomrei Adamah, and COEJL) to promote environmental stewardship; review, evaluate, and improve temple recycling programs and cleaning products where practical; examine food selection and disposal of waste for greening potential; and promote environmental awareness and education throughout the temple community. Each of these goals has been pursued and continues to challenge the community to maintain an ongoing lifestyle of creation care.

The primary, original worship space of the synagogue exhibits a renovated bimah (central elevated platform for reading Torah) reminiscent of a forest setting. The new bimah was installed in the mid-1990s. Tulip poplar wood has been used to create a tall central Torah ark in the shape of a tree trunk. The ark is covered by fabric embroidered with Scripture. Branches stretch out on all sides around the top of the ark. The overall effect resembles a banyan tree and has come to be seen as a tree of life. Carved reading desks flank the ark. Tree stumps, potted plants, and rocks are included as well. Fixed near the top of the ark is a solar-powered *ner tamid.* A dramatic reference to the natural world is sustained and celebrated through this installation.

Temple Emanuel is a partner with Greater Washington Interfaith Power and Light (the benefits of the Interfaith Power and Light network were mentioned in chapter 3). In 2003–2004 the Temple became a partner of the EPA Energy Star Program for Congregations. In 2006 the *Green Shalom Action Guide* was developed as a tool to help promote environmental awareness and education throughout the congregation. Resources of many kinds and practical steps for implementing creation care are contained in the document (available via the temple's website). The congregation has hosted conferences, shared in environmental projects, and developed educational programs to actively engage in creation care through the years.[6]

Robert Schwartz and Keith Peoples of Schwartz and Peoples Architects, Washington, DC, were chosen to assist the congregation with developing expanded spaces for ministry and renovating existing facilities. An addition to the original synagogue structure was planned along with a renovation of the existing building. From the beginning, the congregation and its architects pursued green building, using sustainable principles and products as feasible. The addition and renovation was completed in 2003. The two-story addition included additional classroom and office space, an alternative worship space, a library, and a lobby area. Renovation work was accomplished in the existing school and social hall. Highlights of the addition include minimal disturbance to the building site; orientation of the building to maximize a southern exposure and locating the administrative wing halfway below grade to assist with heating and cooling needs; use of double-glazed, low-E glass; use of renewable or recycled flooring; and the inclusion of high-efficiency lighting. The renovation work included adding new insulation, installing high-efficiency lighting, and modulating the ventilation system for the social hall to reduce its use during periods of low occupancy.

The congregation references the natural world in several ways. An outdoor pavilion provides an alternative setting for worship celebrations. The visual arts and poetry are incorporated into worship to accentuate the beauty of creation and the need to care for it. Religious education activities cultivate the deep connection to environmental care. Children from the congregation have pursued the study of environmental science as a career path. The website of Temple Emmanuel illustrates the commitment of the community to creation care and shares multiple resources with others. "Green Shalom at Temple Emanuel" features the environmental policy of the community, tips for ecologically minded living, *The Green Shalom Guide*, and links to other websites for environmental information and activities. The ways in which the synagogue building embodies creation care are highlighted. In 2005 Temple Emanuel received the Creation Care Award from the National Religious Partnership for the Environment.

ANNUNCIATION OF THE MOTHER OF GOD
BYZANTINE CATHOLIC CHURCH
HOMER GLEN, ILLINOIS
www.byzantinecatholic.com

Annunciation of the Mother of God Byzantine Catholic Church is an Eastern rite congregation located in Homer Glen, west of Chicago. Annunciation Church represents the merging of three ethnically Carpatho-Rusin Greek Catholic congregations in the mid-1990s: St. Mary Assumption Greek Catholic Church of Joliet, Holy Protection of the Blessed Virgin Mary (St. Mary's) Greek Catholic Church of Chicago, and a mission parish of St. Mary's Chicago in Oak Lawn. Father Thomas J. Loya is the current priest for the unified parish and has degrees in both art and theology. He was the priest of St. Mary Assumption in Joliet and facilitated the merger of the three parishes. Ten acres of land were purchased and developed in Homer Glen as a home for the new congregation. The building for the church was completed in 1999.

Environmental stewardship was not in the forefront of the community's mind when its new church was designed and built. Conventional methods for developing the land and constructing the building were used in the original project. In 2002 the surrounding municipality, Homer Township, initiated a community-wide campaign to embody environmental care. Leaders from all quarters of the township were challenged to find ways to pursue creation care. Father Loya thought that environmental stewardship was a public issue that resonated with theological understandings of the church. He and his congregation decided to become a leading voice in their community for creation care in an effort to model their faith convictions and to become better community neighbors. Inspiring others to care for the gift of the earth and facilitating the redemption of destructive patterns of living are two goals of their efforts.

In 2003 Annunciation Church drafted a landscape master plan for redeveloping its ten-acre site. Conservation Design Forum, Elmhurst, Illinois, was retained to develop the master plan for the community. Homer Township was concerned about stormwater management, the flow of rainwater around and through the church's site. In an effort to be a good neighbor, the church kept this important issue in mind and sought to create a beautiful destination for the immediate community that was fully accessible and especially inviting to pedestrians. Father Loya articulated the vision as "a church in a forest preserve." Multiple green features have been developed for three different phases of the master plan. Redeveloping the water detention ponds, introducing natural prairie vegetation, creating pedestrian and bicycle paths to connect with the neighborhood, using permeable pavement, and installing a green roof over the primary building are some of the features of the plan.

Changes favoring natural beauty and healing of the earth are provoking changes to the buildings of Annunciation Church as well. Energy conservation measures, recycling programs, and attention to products used by the faith community are in the works. Pursuing creation care as a faith community is provoking changes in the life patterns of church members. Heightened interest in applying green principles to life outside the church is emerging; for example, choosing high performance energy products, conserving water, and seeking locally grown organic foods. Originally, the local community had resisted the church's plans to locate in Homer Glen. That initial resistance has now turned to affirmation and praise of its presence in the community, and Annunciation Church has received multiple Community in Nature and Harmony awards from the Village of Homer Glen. The visibility of the church and its integral presence as a thoughtful leader in the community is recognized.

PULASKI HEIGHTS UNITED METHODIST CHURCH
LITTLE ROCK, ARKANSAS
www.phumc.com

Pulaski Heights United Methodist Church (PHUMC) was established in 1912 through the efforts of Methodist families meeting under the leadership of Dr. A. C. Miller. Pastor Britt Skarda is the current senior pastor of this congregation of more than four thousand members. The congregation occupied several sites during the first half of the twentieth century, but built its current sanctuary in 1950. The current site they occupy is about 4.75 acres in size. Renovation and expansion projects have been pursued through the years. Today four buildings provide approximately 120,000 square feet of space. Pursuing green building strategies for future projects emerged as a priority in 1999 as a new building committee was formed and began to dream. One of the members was an architect who helped the group become aware of the creation care potential of sustainable design. The committee generated a master plan outlining a long-range plan, which was approved by the congregation in 2001. Phase one of the project was to include a new multipurpose building, a parking deck, and a columbarium. Phase two was to include renovating the Norma Story building, music areas, offices, classrooms, and reception area and creating new offices, classrooms, and atrium space. The approximate cost for phase one was set at just under $10 million. A decision was made by the building committee to pursue LEED certification for the new multipurpose building. Cromwell Architects Engineers, Little Rock, Arkansas, was selected to design and construct the new facilities.

Ground was broken for the first phase of the master plan in October 2003. The new multipurpose building, the Victor H.

Nixon Disciple Center, opened in 2005. The Gothic-style architecture of the surrounding church buildings, which was popular
among faith communities in the United States from the nineteenth to the mid-twentieth centuries, was retained in the exterior of the new building. The new center incorporates this style
through the use of brick, cast stone dressings, buttresses, and two-
centered, three-centered, and lancet arches. The three-story center
(38,000 square feet) is designed to accommodate multiple ministries, especially youth and educational activities. Wesley Hall, a
four-hundred-seat multipurpose room with complete audiovisual
system, accommodates worship celebrations and other events. A
labyrinth, used for devotional purposes, is embedded in the car-
peted surface of Wesley Hall. In June 2004 the Nixon Disciple
Center became the first church building to be registered for LEED
certification in the state of Arkansas. In January 2006 the building
was certified by LEED.

The pursuit of LEED certification for the Nixon Center had a
profound effect on the creation care awareness and efforts of the
congregation. In December 2005 a Green Team was established to
assist with promoting the awareness of creation care throughout
the congregation. Subsequent renovation and expansion work on
existing buildings in phase two of the master plan (2006–2007) included green features such as incorporating additional insulation,
high-efficiency HVAC, high-efficiency lighting, high-efficiency
windows (double glazed and gas filled, with low-E glass and insulated frames), and low-flow water fixtures and using building
materials with recycled content. In April 2007 a seven-week study
for adults, "Caring for God's Earth," was conducted by the leadership of the Green Team. In June 2008 the Green Team organized
a conference at the church for all communities of faith in the area
that might be interested in initiating their own creation care efforts. In April 2009 the team established an electronic recycling
drop-off site at the church.

PHUMC hosted a faith-based, statewide conference concerning religion, justice, and the environment in May 2009. Christian
and Jewish leaders delivered keynote addresses. At the conference
an initiative was introduced to establish an Arkansas affiliate of the

Interfaith Power and Light network. In August 2009 the PHUMC Green Team was awarded the Conservationist Organization of the Year award from the Arkansas Wildlife Federation. Founding members of the Green Team were involved in establishing both the Arkansas affiliate of the Interfaith Power and Light network and the Arkansas Green Faith Alliance, efforts recognized by an award from the Arkansas chapter of the Sierra Club in 2010.

The church website has a "Caring for Creation" entry under the "Resources, Missions" tab on its home page. The section describes opportunities for sharing in the work of the PHUMC Green Team, Green Faith Alliance of Central Arkansas, and the Arkansas chapter of Interfaith Power and Light. Ongoing opportunities for the congregation to share in the work of creation care are available in this way.

HISTORIC PRESERVATION CONSTRUCTION PROJECTS

MUSEUM AT ELDRIDGE STREET AND ELDRIDGE STREET SYNAGOGUE
NEW YORK CITY
www.eldridgestreet.org
National Historic Landmark, 1996

The Eldridge Street Synagogue was built by Congregation Kahal Adath Jeshurun, a community affiliated with the Orthodox tradition (today, the Union of Orthodox Jewish Congregations of America).[7] Significant immigration of Jews from Eastern Europe to New York City occurred in the latter part of the nineteenth century. Eldridge Street Synagogue became an important center of faith and social activities for these early immigrants. The property is composed of three adjacent lots (together the lots cover an area approximately sixty feet long by eighty-seven and one half feet deep) on Eldridge Street on the Lower East Side in the borough of Manhattan.

Roman Catholic, German immigrant architects Peter and Francis Herter were selected to design the synagogue (their only synagogue project). The building is three stories tall and has a full basement. The architectural style of the design is eclectic: Gothic influence is present in the use of twin towers surrounding a central bay with a rose window; Romanesque influence can be discerned in the majority of the masonry; and Moorish influences are evident in the use of horseshoe arches on the exterior and interior and in decorative elements in the building. Construction of the building began in September 1886 and was completed by September 1887. The building's foundation walls are made of stone. Wood girders and joists and brick masonry walls are used for the primary structure. The roof is slate. Two rows of wood columns are incorporated to provide additional support. The original cost of the building, both for the land and to build, was $92,000. Gas fixtures were initially used throughout the building but were upgraded to electric in the early 1900s. The faith commitment, sacrifices, and efforts of many Eastern European immigrants made the synagogue possible. The building was designated a National Historic Landmark on the National Register of Historic Places in 1996.

The Eldridge Street Synagogue community was at its most active from 1887 to the 1920s. Various factors influenced a decline in the congregation from the mid-1920s to 1940s, including members' moving out of the community as they grew in affluence, passage of the Immigration Act of 1924 that limited the number of incoming immigrants, and the Great Depression. Also, following World War II, a building boom led to an urban exodus. Many people left the city and built new synagogues in the suburbs. By the 1950s the congregation was no longer regularly using the primary worship space due to increasing maintenance needs and low attendance, and the small congregation met in the basement for worship. Deterioration of the building continued into the 1980s. In 1986 a nonsectarian, not-for-profit organization, Eldridge Street Project, was established to restore the synagogue and provide educational and cultural programs about the immigrant experience. In 1990 architect Jill H. Gotthelf (then with Robert E. Meadows, PC, Architects in New York) developed a master plan to restore the synagogue. Gotthelf, now with Walter Sedovic Architects in Irvington-on-Hudson, New York, remained with the project for more than sixteen years. Green building design principles were infused into the master plan.

In December 2007 restoration of the Eldridge Street Synagogue was completed for a total investment of $18.5 million. Preservation and green design have been achieved in tandem in multiple ways. Restoring the synagogue is itself a primary way to pursue sustainable building. Renewing the building reduces the need for site development, material use, and waste production. Several features were originally designed into the synagogue that are considered green options today: operable stained-glass windows for ventilation and cooling of the sanctuary in the summer; skylights and clerestories to maximize natural light; and use of durable materials such as stone and brick to extend the usable life of the building and reduce building waste. Salvaged materials from the original building and nearby sources—including stained glass, wood, and brass fixtures—were at times used in the project. New building materials included recycled content, such as discarded plastic for counters and stall dividers in bathrooms, discarded blue jeans in insulation, and fly ash (a waste product from steel production) in the concrete. Lime mortar, a very old and durable material, rather than concrete, was used to repoint the façade. Salvaged pavers were also used for repaving certain areas.

A small group of believers composes the current faith community, Congregation Kahal Adath Jeshurun with Anshe Lubz. The congregation continues to use the synagogue for regular services, but the building is administered and operated by the Eldridge Street Project. In 2008 Eldridge Street Project changed its name to the Museum at Eldridge Street. The museum documents and celebrates the history and accomplishments of this faith community and the Jewish immigrant experience in America through its tours, interactive exhibits, and active calendar of events for people of all faiths and cultural backgrounds.

The restoration work to Eldridge Street Synagogue has won recognition for its environmental intentions and beauty. A few of its honors include National Trust for Historic Preservation's

2008 Preservation Honor Award; Metropolitan Chapter of the
Victorian Society in America Restoration Award; Municipal Art
Society's Masterwork Award for New York City's Best Restoration
Project; and New York Landmarks Conservancy Lucy G. Moses
Preservation Award. Evidence of historic evolution and use remain, such as the bare bulbs encircling the board that exhibits the
Ten Commandments, nineteenth-century gas fixtures, and worn
grooves in the wooden floorboards of the sanctuary. And new life
continues. Artist Kiki Smith and architect Deborah Gans designed
a rose window to replace the original stained glass window, which
was damaged beyond repair and replaced by glass block in 1944.
No records of the original window could be found, so a new design was commissioned. The window features a central Star of
David in a field of blue surrounded by yellow five-pointed stars.
The building shares in celebrating the faith, history, and piety of
the community in ways that support creation care.

UNITY TEMPLE UNITARIAN UNIVERSALIST CONGREGATION
OAK PARK, ILLINOIS
www.unitytemple.org, www.unitytemple-utrf.org
National Historic Landmark, 1970

Unity Church, originally established as an independent liberal congregation, was founded in the village of Oak Park near Chicago
in 1871.[8] In time the church affiliated with the Unitarian denomi-
nation. In 1961 Unity Church became the Unitarian Universalist
Church in Oak Park. In 1994 the congregation united with Beacon
Unitarian Church, Oak Park, to become Unity Temple Unitarian
Universalist Congregation. The congregation includes about five
hundred people today. The Reverend Alan Taylor is the present
senior pastor. The church is located on a long and narrow lot (approximately four-tenths of an acre) on a busy corner.

In 1905 the original building for Unity Temple was destroyed
by fire, and the community decided to rebuild. They selected an
architect familiar with their congregation, Frank Lloyd Wright
(1867–1959), to design the new building. Wright had become an
innovative and recognized architect by the turn of the century. He

was developing a contemporary style of design that would come to be called "prairie style." In keeping with the spirit of Unitarianism, Wright sought to create a meeting place for the faith community to gather, worship, and work that was focused on the divine among people. The overall design of the church features two primary spaces: a space for public worship, Unity Temple, and a space for social service, Unity House. A spacious entry hall joins the two spaces. Offices, classrooms, and various meeting rooms are found in the buildings. Wright also designed interior features, including light fixtures, windows, and skylights for the buildings. The worship space is nearly thirty feet high and has seating for 345 people, with seats distributed over three levels on three sides of the central pulpit area. No worshiper is more than forty-five feet away from the speaker. Clerestory windows (some of which can be opened for natural ventilation) and laylights (with skylights above them for weather protection), displaying Wright's abstract glass designs, allow much natural light into the space.

Unity Temple was built between 1906 and 1908 for about $60,000 (one-third over the original budget). The prairie-style building emphasizes the horizontal plane over the vertical, incorporates large overhangs, uses limited angular ornamentation on the exterior, and includes integrated plantings. Poured-in-place concrete (with steel reinforcement) was the primary building material for the project, an emerging material and process for public buildings at that time. In both design and material choice, Unity Temple was a significant departure from traditional ecclesiastical architecture. Unity Temple was recognized as an early pioneer in modern American church design. Its significance was acknowledged through its inclusion on the National Register for Historic Places as a National Historic Landmark in December 1970.

New, untested building materials and processes inevitably provide maintenance challenges over time. The poured concrete of Unity Temple has yielded cracks and failed to maintain its integrity through the years. No expansion joints were included in the design, and the flat roofs have been found to have inadequate drainage systems. Water has taken a significant toll on the building. In an effort to preserve the original integrity of the building for the congregation and surrounding community, the Unity Temple Restoration Foundation, a nonsectarian, nonprofit organization was created in 1973. Harboe Architects, Chicago, was appointed as preservation architect by Unity Temple Restoration Foundation to develop a plan to restore the building. The current restoration master plan, developed in 2006, divides the restoration into three phases: structural stabilization, interior climate control and mechanical systems, and interior restoration. A comprehensive restoration of Unity Temple is estimated to cost approximately $20 to $25 million. One-half million dollars was raised by Unity Temple Restoration Foundation and the congregation in 2009 to do emergency stabilization work to a portion of the concrete roof. The State of Illinois, Save America's Treasures at the National Park Service, the National Trust for Historic Preservation, and other sources have donated financial resources for the restoration work. In 2009 the National Trust for Historic Preservation named Unity Temple one of their eleven most endangered places worthy of immediate attention. As funding is available, the needed work is being completed.

Unity Temple has an active congregation that has been intentional about its commitment to sustainable living for the last ten years. Under the leadership of their Green Sanctuary Committee, members have examined the ecological footprint of their community and completed an energy audit to apply for recognition as an official Green Sanctuary congregation in the Unitarian Universalist Association. These activities helped them identify ways in which they could become more sustainable. Numerous efforts to increase energy efficiency, promote recycling, and pursue responsible purchasing have been achieved. Creation care is celebrated in thematic ways and through special worship services. They coordinate a worship event with Earth Day each year and have occasional "car free" Sundays to encourage walking, bicycling, and use of mass transit. Activities for all ages are organized to teach the principles and patterns of sustainable living. They have conducted congregational surveys, for youth and adults, about environmental awareness and hosted film showings and group discussions on topics such as waste disposal, sustainable living, and solar energy. Environmental justice is pursued through support of Unity Temple's community minister, the Reverend Clare Butterfield, who directs Faith in Place (www.faithinplace.org). Faith in Place, initiated by Butterfield in 1999, is a partnership of more than six hundred congregations in Illinois, from many religious traditions, committed to creation care. They are also part of the national Interfaith Power and Light campaign. Sustainable living initiatives, congregational education, advocacy for environmental issues, and networking for ideas and support are all pursued through this organization.

CONCLUSIONS

All types of congregational building projects can incorporate creation care into their vision and plans. Both land and buildings hold potential for achieving green initiatives. Congregations today are realizing that that they can take an active role in caring for the ground they occupy, for their own good and for the good of their neighbors. While some congregations have experienced opposition to their presence in a location because they will not add to a local tax base, the pursuit of good land and building stewardship can contribute in multiple ways to the surrounding community. The congregations featured here illustrate how storm-water management, land restoration, recreation areas, and support of the local economy can be addressed as dimensions of creation care to the benefit of the wider community. A commitment to green building can be initiated at any time in the lifespan of a congregation. The range of options for sustainable design will vary according to a range of variables, but the option to explore and change incrementally is always open.

Congregations that exhibit creation care in and through their property and buildings generally have leaders who are committed to integrating environmental responsibility into the life of the community. Creation care is not a stand-alone pursuit, nor is it a transitory concern. Several of the leaders of the congregations profiled in this chapter acknowledged that environmental steward-ship is not a passing fad but an important dimension of living that should be integrated into daily life, corporately and individually. A vision for creation care and a long-term action plan are both required. Over time the initiatives become natural rhythms for life rather than extraordinary measures. Recycling is an example of this phenomenon. While separating trash requires more effort when a community begins a recycling program (for example, tak-ing waste to special facilities), citywide initiatives can eventually become commonplace and establish new patterns for waste dis-posal, including curbside pickup. The more congregations engage in behavior-changing policies in support of environmental stew-ardship, the more related choices will become ordinary. And be-cause the culture around us is more keenly aware of environmental concerns today, people who would like to contribute to sustain-able living are sometimes attracted to green congregations as well.

The next chapters will investigate more specific ways in which congregations can fulfill creation care through green building. Chapter 5 will discuss the land, chapter 6 will consider the build-ing shell, and chapter 7 will examine the interior environment. Specific aspects of building will be illustrated through the variety of ways in which the congregations featured here worked with their property.

CHAPTER 5

The Land We Occupy

We often take land for granted. As we go about our daily routines—
in houses, schools, and workplaces—we rarely give much thought
to nurturing the ground beneath our feet. It would be important
to begin this consideration of land by remembering that the land
comes to us as a gift from God and our very existence depends on
this gift. As created beings, we are both derived from land or soil
and completely dependent on it for life. We read in Genesis that
God formed us from the dust of the earth. In a sense, we are one
with the earth itself. And God intended the first people on earth
to be sustained by the resources of the physical earth, especially
its soil, water, and plant life. The land is our source of life and is
entrusted to our care.

Farmers, landscapers, earthmovers, or others whose vocation
directly involves soil tend to be more aware of our relationship
to the land. They learn to evaluate the quality of the land. They
are aware of its condition and of the interdependency that exists
between the land and a myriad of life forms (human, animal, and
plant). In caring for the land, we are ultimately caring for all of
these life forms. Today, those of us with a Western mindset practice ways of life that often distance us from concerns for the land;
therefore we have to be more intentional about not taking soil for

granted. The property we choose to occupy for our faith communities presents an opportunity to remember the land and to express creation care. Decisions about site selection, storm-water management, heat island effect, site lighting, and transportation to and from a site will be examined in this chapter.

INITIAL SITE SELECTION

Site selection is an early occasion in the building or renovating process for exercising creation care. Concerns have been raised in recent decades about the rate at which previously untouched natural habitat is being developed. The term *sprawl* has emerged in architectural circles to describe what appears to be unreflective, rapid consumption of undeveloped land for residential and commercial building. At its worst, sprawl is a pattern of consumer behavior in which the land itself is viewed as nothing more than a disposable commodity. Entire natural ecosystems can be drastically altered through this type of growth. And unintended consequences, such as increasing distances between important destinations, result that predispose us to rely upon limited forms of transport. Some communities have implemented or are considering "smart growth" principles, establishing urban growth boundaries that restrict the expansion of suburban and urban development. In areas governed by smart growth, emphasis is placed on more compact urban development. Smart growth could yield more stewardship-oriented design of suburban and urban areas. Congregations need to begin thinking more intentionally about how the building we pursue contributes to the growth patterns of the communities in which we live.

In land development circles, property for building can be categorized as *greenfield* or *brownfield*. Previously undeveloped land (or land used only for agricultural purposes) is called *greenfield property*. Greenfield sites are usually located on the edges of towns and cities. They are attractive for their pristine condition and usually less expensive price tag due the lack of infrastructure (access, utilities, and so forth). It is possible to practice creation care in and through a greenfield site by minimally affecting the land being developed and by preserving existing habitat. For many communities, selecting a greenfield site will be a good option.

Greenfield sites that have already been developed are an important option to consider too. Initial development of a greenfield site requires time, energy, and resources to provide the necessary infrastructure for building. Land grading, transport connections, and electrical, communication, water, and waste disposal systems all need to be established. Significant material and financial resources will be required. Redeveloping existing building sites does not incur these initial costs or contribute to expanding development boundaries.

A second type of site is available for faith communities to occupy as well: *brownfield property*. Brownfield land is property that was previously developed for industrial or certain commercial purposes but has since been abandoned or is being underutilized. The definition applies to property that was used for specific purposes. Not all previously used property is called brownfield. Redeveloping brownfield land requires addressing real or perceived environmental contamination. Often financial incentives are made available via federal, state, or city sources to encourage people to occupy and transform brownfield sites. In theological terms, brownfield land is truly in need of redemption. Careful analysis of a particular site's profile would need to be conducted before attempting to transform a brownfield site for congregational uses, but such an act would be a profound statement of commitment to creation care. And collateral benefits for transforming the surrounding community could follow this type of restoration.

LAND STEWARDSHIP IN THE SUBURBS

Keystone Community Church, Ada, Michigan, purchased an undeveloped thirty-five-acre site adjacent to a residential area in a suburb of Grand Rapids. It originally had rolling hills, heavy woods, a meadow, and wetlands. The site was carefully analyzed prior to building. A commitment to creation care from the start resulted in minimal disturbance of the site during building. Keystone preserved natural elements, performed minimal grading, and provided open space. The building and parking areas were located on an existing elevated meadow, which meant that little soil and few trees needed to be moved. The heavy woods on the north side of the site near the auditorium were retained. Their presence helps to mitigate the effects of the prevailing cold winter winds on the building and provides a vista of beauty.

Minimizing Site Disturbance

Reducing disturbance to a building site can include the following:

- Preserving natural elements
- Minimizing land grading
- Minimizing building and parking areas
- Utilizing native and noninvasive (adaptive) plantings in landscape design
- Providing open space for natural habitat

Vegetative bioswales were created on the site to facilitate storm-water management. Roads, parking areas, and roofs are surfaces that do not absorb water. When rain falls and flows across these surfaces, it is called storm-water runoff. This runoff water picks up pollutants such as gasoline, oil, and heavy metals that gather on these artificial surfaces. Runoff water can also pick up fertilizers and other chemicals that we use to treat our agricultural acreage, lawns, groundcover, and other plantings. As our built environment (buildings and transportation infrastructure) ages its components can leech chemical contamination as well. Bioswales and wetlands can be created to help direct, detain, and process this excess water and are often located along roadsides, next to parking lots, or between developed properties. The subsoil of the bioswales can include soil, sand, gravel, rock, and organic materials. Vegetation and the organisms that live in a well-maintained bioswale filter soil sediment and other pollutants out of the water.

Four hundred linear feet of swale on the Keystone site feed into a ten-thousand-square-foot constructed wetland, another vegetative area intended to retain water over an extended period. The wetland continues the filtration process and protects against erosion by allowing storm water to absorb slowly into the earth. Water moves through the wetlands area and ultimately into a 0.78-acre retention pond. Storm-water management is a significant issue in an environment of pavement and roofing, and faith communities can provide important modeling through bioswale and wetland development.

Erosion and sedimentation were also controlled in the development of Keystone. Often when land is disturbed by construction, soil—including valuable topsoil—is exposed, displaced, and then lost as ground is stripped of vegetation, manipulated, and subject to rain and wind. Laying soil erosion matting (organic materials woven into temporary protective covers), seeding disturbed areas, maintaining natural buffers (leaving land undisturbed) along property lines, and preserving existing vegetation all help minimize erosion and soil degradation. The natural integrity and beauty of the land we occupy can be retained by limiting the impact of our development efforts.

Landscape choices at Keystone favored indigenous (native to that region), drought-resistant plants so that landscaped areas would not need to be irrigated. They also chose noninvasive (not a threat to native species), drought-resistant species to complement indigenous choices. Some noninvasive species are long-adapted to areas and can work well with indigenous plantings. Areas in front of the building exhibit ornamental grasses, native wildflowers, and stones and boulders. Turf grass includes low maintenance, drought-tolerant seed and native wildflowers. The parking area is planted with drought-tolerant deciduous and evergreen trees to provide both beauty and shade for the pavement.

Light pollution is a reality that often goes unrecognized. Keystone chose low energy exterior lighting fixtures that focus light downward. The lighting is controlled by a combination of light sensors and computer systems designed to maintain the lowest level of lighting possible while observing limits of safety. In this way, the beauty of the night is enhanced and adequate illumination is provided at minimal energy cost.

Curbing Excess Exterior Light at Night

Limiting the potential for light pollution includes the following:

- Determining the minimal amount of light necessary for safety at night in areas outside the building(s)
- Using low-wattage bulbs for light fixtures
- Shielding exterior fixtures of more than fifty watts, which direct the lighting to the needed area
- Using renewable energy sources for light fixtures
- Installing automatic controllers to limit interior lighting that may be visible outside

Transportation is a final consideration in site development. Transportation to a building is an important, if often overlooked, source of energy consumption. For example, in office buildings, the energy expended by employees who commute to a building on a given day can be more than twice the energy expended for building operations.[1] Encouraging shared rides and alternative forms of transportation can have a significant impact on creation care. Keystone accommodates automobile transportation but chose to encourage carpooling and electric vehicles. Special parking spaces are set aside for those who carpool and those who use electric cars. Bike racks and showering facilities for cyclists were installed to encourage bicycle use. Efforts to accommodate and encourage alternative transportation options can help our communities achieve more sustainable modes of transport.

LAND IN TRUST FOR CONGREGATION AND COMMUNITY

Congregation Beth David, San Luis Obispo, California, has had a long-standing commitment to care for its land in responsible ways and searched a long time for the right property. The primary force for building a new synagogue was the need for facility expansion. But a growing desire to embody the Jewish concept of *tikkun olam* (repairing the world) led to the ultimate selection of an undeveloped ninety-two-acre site just outside the city limits. An early decision was made to use only a fraction of the property for the building and parking, and the community chose to develop thirteen acres. Sixty-two acres were set aside for wetland preservation, agriculture, and open space in an effort to treasure and preserve the surrounding natural landscape. They initiated a detailed examination of the site, which noted the natural topography and features, vegetation, and wildlife. Extensive data was collected on local weather conditions, including the amount of sunlight throughout the year, rainfall, and prevailing seasonal winds. The observations led to a more thoughtful relationship between the congregation and its land and yielded important insights that guided decisions concerning site development, landscaping choices, and renewable energy potential.

Minimal disturbance of the thirteen acres was a goal. Measures were taken to minimize erosion and sediment production. In addition to leveling the site, the congregation created a ten-foot-high berm along the side of the parking lot that flanks the highway to the city. The berm was landscaped in indigenous, drought-resistant plantings and serves as a barrier from traffic noise and headlight glare. It also provides protection from the prevailing winds. Native drought-resistant plants were also used in landscaping around the building and parking area. A recovery program for Congdon's Tarplant, a threatened plant species found on the site, was even established. Barn owls are indigenous to the area and, in an effort to encourage their presence, nesting boxes were installed. The owls serve a helpful role in providing natural pest control around the synagogue. Bioswales were incorporated at Beth David, as at Keystone, to facilitate storm-water management.

The congregation also considered transportation to and from the site. Most people come to the synagogue by automobile, and the primary entrance to the site is from an adjacent highway, with parking provided alongside the ten-foot high berm. The synagogue provides priority parking for carpooling. Bicyclists are accommodated as well with facilities for parking bicycles. Two bus lines adjacent to the property entrance provide convenient access to public transportation.

CHURCH IN A FOREST PRESERVE

Annunciation of the Mother of God Byzantine Catholic Church, Homer Glen, Illinois, established a vision for gradually transforming its property according to environmentally sustainable ideals. The ten-acre site is surrounded by residential properties. The original sculpting of the site and landscaping favored grass turf lawns and ornamental plantings not native to the area; and a rigorous program of maintenance— including cutting, trimming, watering, and fertilizing—was required to maintain the plantings. A combination of factors provoked the community to rethink its original landscape choices. The township had issued a call to property owners to consider more sustainable ways of building and maintaining property. Leaders of the church had been interested in creation care and decided to accept this invitation from the town's leaders, in part to model the connection between their faith and environmental stewardship. Sustainable strategies for landscaping emerged as an important new priority for the church.

In consultation with others, congregational leaders realized that they could reduce or eliminate the need to water, reduce or eliminate the need for commercial fertilizer, and promote indigenous plant species on their site. They also learned that storm-water management was an issue for the adjacent neighborhoods.

A master plan was adopted that would accommodate and filter storm water from the surrounding area and allow for a transition to plantings that would be in keeping with the native biology of the region. Vegetative swales and wetlands were constructed in the front half of the property. A planted detention pond is on one side of the property, surrounded by footpaths and the occasional bench for sitting. The paths that cross the church property allow pedestrians to reach adjacent properties. Various indigenous species of grasses, trees, and wildflowers are located throughout the landscape. Different zones are planted with varieties that thrive according to the varying moisture levels found within the swales and wetlands. A portion of the property is planted as prairie restoration. (More will be said about this below in the section "Restoration and Regeneration of the Land.") Additional prairie restoration and further adjustments to the landscaping may be pursued in the future as funding is available.

Annunciation Church's storm-water management pond surrounded by prairie restoration plantings. The small footbridge on the right of the photograph is part of a walking path across the church property. (Author photo.)

Insects and animals native to the restored habitat, including but-terflies, herons, and bluebirds, are returning to the area. Nesting boxes have been set up to provide an additional incentive for blue-birds to return. Through the efforts of the Annunciation commu-nity, members and visitors now feel like they are in a more rural setting in the midst of this residential area. The overall impression is one of peace and beauty. Father Loya has expressed a desire for Annunciation Church to be thought of as "a church in a forest preserve." The community is on its way to achieving this vision.

Storm water is to be managed in other ways as well, accord-ing to their multiphase master plan. A green roof is planned for the primary church building. Green roofs are composed of layers of vegetation, engineered soil, and a waterproof membrane. The green roof absorbs water from rain and acts as a first filter for the water. At Annunciation Church the water from the roof will be directed into two adjacent features. A water garden planted with lilies, arrowhead, pickerelweed, and rushes is to be located near the entrance drive to the building complex. And a water terrace will be installed on another side of the church. The water fea-tures will beautify the building complex and provide locations for contemplation, prayer, and celebrations. Green roofs also enhance air quality (plants absorb carbon dioxide and release oxygen) and provide a natural form of insulation for the building.

Paved areas were not overlooked. The primary entrance drive at Annunciation Church is made with permeable pavement mate-rial, allowing water to be absorbed into the ground beneath the drive. Plans are underway to transition the existing parking area to permeable pavement as well. A variety of designs and materials are available today for creating permeable drives and parking surfac-es, and a small portion of the rear parking area is currently being tested to determine the best solution for their particular setting.

Storm-water Management Strategies

Measures for storm-water management include use of the following:

- Vegetative bioswales
- Constructed wetlands
- Rainwater gardens
- Green roofs
- Permeable roadway or parking area materials

Many of the measures useful for storm-water management have a collateral benefit: combating a phenomenon called "heat island effect." Buildings and traditionally paved areas absorb, store, and radiate heat. Anyone who has walked across a large paved parking area on a hot summer day is familiar with this phenomenon. Urban areas generally have temperatures slightly higher than rural areas due to their greater degree of development. These increased temperatures result in increased energy consumption in summer months (to provide additional cooling), which elevates emissions of air pollutants and greenhouse gases. Even runoff rainwater can be affected. As water is exposed to buildings and pavement, it absorbs some of their heat and transfers this heat to aquatic environments. The increased heat can stress natural habitats. The projected green roof and existing permeable paving of Annunciation Church will provide cooler surfaces and reduce heat island effect on its site. Plantings of all kinds naturally mitigate heat island effect, too, a feature that many of the congregations discussed here exhibit.

RESTORATION AND REGENERATION OF THE LAND

Implementing creation care principles for site development can range from minimizing one's impact on the land to actually helping the land become healthier than it is today. Restorating and regenerating a piece of property is a long-term commitment to environmental stewardship. The Benedictine Women of Madison exhibit this long-term commitment in their gradual development of the site occupied by Holy Wisdom Monastery in Middleton, Wisconsin. The original forty-two-acre site the community purchased in 1953 has grown, through gradual acquisitions, to include 138 acres today. Much of the additional property had been farmland that surrounded the site. In consultation with others, Holy Wisdom developed a master plan in 1995 for restoring the site to natural upland prairie, the original planting of the area. Prairie restoration is helpful for multiple reasons: restoring indigenous plant life; attracting indigenous wildlife, including birds and insects for pollinating; preserving topsoil; rebuilding the nutrient content of soil; and increasing water absorption capacity. Natural prairie does need some maintenance, such as occasional burning and weeding, but supplemental water, fertilizer treatments, and frequent cutting (as with turf grass) are unnecessary.

The women of Holy Wisdom are keenly aware of the importance of community, and they have developed a network of volunteers who share a passion for cultivating a healthy earth and a vision for restoring the land. Volunteers include those who have experienced the spiritual retreats the community regularly offers, members of the local parish that meets at the monastery, and interested people in the surrounding area. Each year volunteers gather periodically to gather and sow indigenous flower and grass seeds for restoring the prairie. In 1998 this project received the Wisconsin Business Friend of the Environment Award. Insight from environmental consultants at the nearby campus of the University of Wisconsin in Madison was sought as well, an effort that yielded both information about creation care and internship opportunities for students pursuing environmental studies. Ninety-five of the 138 acres have been restored to date, and four trails ranging from 0.3 to 2.0 miles in length have been created to allow those on retreat or from the surrounding community to enjoy the flora and fauna of the monastery. A trail map and guide to the grounds has been developed for visitors.

From 1997 to 1999 the restoration work included dredging Lost Lake, a ten-thousand-year-old glacial lake. The lake, originally nine acres in surface area, had been reduced to less than two acres through the years due to sediment buildup caused by local farming practices and residential development. Eighty-five thousand cubic yards of silt were removed, and the lake now detains and filters water runoff for two hundred surrounding acres. This restoration work was designated a demonstration project of the Lake Mendota Priority Watershed in 1996, received a Yahara Lakes Association Certificate of Appreciation in 1997, and received the Dane County Waters Champion Award in 2005.

Other features that have been incorporated into the property include green or vegetative roofing on two portions of the new monastery building, permeable concrete for parking areas, and rain gardens and rain barrels to maximize the benefits of rainwater. Rain gardens located adjacent to the building and parking area provide additional plantings and detain and filter storm water runoff. Rain barrels are used so that no additional irrigation is needed for any of the plantings. The efforts of Holy Wisdom have reduced the storm-water runoff by a remarkable 13 percent over the predevelopment capacity of the property. When the cumulative effects of improving the soil content through prairie restoration, dredging Lost Lake, and managing storm-water runoff are combined, the community has moved beyond "sustainable" on the greening scale to "restorative and regenerative." Holy Wisdom is not simply minimizing its impact on the earth but is also improving the land and leaving it healthier than it was when the community first occupied the property.

Heat island effect is countered at Holy Wisdom in several ways. While a portion of the roof is a "green roof," others are "cool," meaning they are covered with highly reflective material that reduces heat absorption from the sun. The many plantings on the property and the use of permeable paving for parking and highly reflective pavers for walkways all help reduce heat island effect.

Measures to Prevent Heat Island Effect

Reducing heat island effect can be achieved by the following:

- Planting trees and other vegetative covers
- Minimizing building and pavement surface areas

- Using permeable paving materials for drives and parking areas
- Installing green roofs
- Installing reflective materials on roof surfaces
- Using reflective pavement materials for walkways

EXAMPLES FROM OTHER PROJECTS

St. Gabriel of the Sorrowful Virgin Church, Toronto, Ontario, has incorporated underground parking for more than one hundred vehicles into its site. Using less pavement reduces the potential for storm-water runoff and the generation of additional heat (thus reducing heat island effect). A small parking area is available next to the church building for those with disabilities, those who carpool, and those who drive hybrid vehicles. Provision is also made for electric vehicles and those who ride bicycles. An extensive garden is located on the south side of the church building. The garden, visible from the primary sanctuary through a glass curtain wall (nonloadbearing wall), has drought-resistant plantings. Rainwater from the building roof is directed to a cistern, which is connected to a drip irrigation system that serves the garden. People coming from the underground lot are guided to exit into this garden or to a stairway passage featuring an interior vertical garden (more will be said of this feature in chapter 7).

Not all faith communities have a large site with which to work. Jewish Reconstructionist Community, Evanston, Illinois, has a small corner site in an urban setting. The synagogue building takes up the majority of the site, with indigenous and adaptive drought-resistant plant species surrounding the structure. The landscaping does not need to be irrigated. A playground area next to the synagogue incorporates mulch from recycled rubber tires. A small parking lot has been established just across the street from the building, but the property is located near mass transit lines, therefore using public transportation is encouraged. Carpoolers are rewarded with access to specially designated parking spaces, and each light fixture for the parking area is powered via a solar panel. Bicycle riding is encouraged through the provision of facilities to accommodate both bikes and riders.

Transportation Considerations

Congregations can encourage alternative transportation by

- Selecting a site with access to mass transit lines (such as bus, subway, or rail)
- Developing connections to adjacent properties and communities via walkways and paths for pedestrian and bicycle transport
- Providing storage for bicycles (outdoor or indoor; racks, lockers, or rooms) and bathing facilities for bike riders
- Providing preferred parking for those who carpool
- Offering preferred parking for alternative-energy vehicles (such as electric or hybrid vehicles)
- Designating short-term parking areas "no-idle zones"
- Minimizing the size of the parking area to encourage mass transit use or carpooling

---

Temple Emanuel, Kensington, Maryland, occupies a five-acre parcel of land. Their project involved an expansion of their facility. Care was taken to only minimally disturb the site. The portion of the new building that houses the administrative offices was located half below grade, taking advantage of the thermal properties of the earth itself for temperature control. A comprehensive landscaping plan was developed for the synagogue site. Drought-resistant indigenous plants were selected to help restore native habitat and limit dependency on supplemental water. Alternate transportation was emphasized by including facilities for bicyclists.

Pulaski Heights United Methodist Church, Little Rock, Arkansas, also expanded its campus. In building their new structure and renovating existing buildings, they were careful to avoid dumping as much waste as possible in landfills (including 75 percent of their new construction waste). Reducing heat island effect was achieved through minimizing parking areas, using reflective material on the roof of the new building, and landscaping with drought-tolerant plantings and drip irrigation. The congregation planned the expansion to encourage congregants' use of existing public transportation and bicycles instead of automobiles.

Pulaski Heights United Methodist Church's multistory parking deck, under construction, in close proximity to the church's new and existing buildings. Minimizing the paved area reduces both heat island effect and the development of additional property. (Photo provided by Pulaski Heights UMC; used with permission.)

WORKING WITH THE LAND

The congregations examined here exhibit a range of thoughtful choices that affect site selection and development. Keystone

Church and Annunciation Church chose greenfield sites located in residential areas. Congregation Beth David and the Holy Wisdom community chose greenfield land outside of urban or suburban confines. Keystone Church and Congregation Beth David respected the existing natural ecosystem of the property from the inception of their projects. Buildings were situated to minimize site disturbance and to take advantage of existing natural features. Annunciation Church chose a redevelopment strategy that sought restoration of the native habitat. The Holy Wisdom community minimally developed their original site and tripled the size of the property over time. Continuing care over decades has resulted in not only restoration of the natural habitat of their property but also regeneration such that its level of health continues to improve.

Jewish Reconstructionist Congregation (JRC), St. Gabriel Church, Temple Emanuel, and Pulaski Heights Church chose to renew their land in conjunction with a building project. Existing buildings can be replaced, as in the examples of JRC and St. Gabriel Church, and even Holy Wisdom did this. Or existing buildings can be renovated and expanded, as did Temple Emanuel and Pulaski Heights Church. Each of these communities took care to create minimal disturbance of the site during their development, diverted as much material as possible from landfills, and implemented new landscape designs. Attention to indigenous and drought-resistant plantings helped to restore the natural flora and fauna of the area and reduce the amount of water needed for maintenance. Historical buildings can also limit site disturbance, divert construction waste from landfills, and pursue renewed landscape designs in their preservation work.

CHAPTER 6

The Buildings We Use

The building shell presents numerous challenges related to environmental stewardship for each faith community. The building shell, or envelope, is the basic structure of a building—the foundation, floors, walls, roof, windows, and doors. The building shell serves multiple functions: stability, protection from weather, a noise barrier, protection from intruders (including insects and other wildlife), and security for occupants and assets. Multiple factors affect the design of the shell for a church: historical patterns for religious spaces, the design patterns of the surrounding community, current aesthetic movements in the wider culture, aesthetic preferences of the faith community, aesthetic preferences of the designer, limits imposed by building materials, and budget constraints. Materials used for the building shell often include wood, glass, metal, brick, stone, and concrete. Synthetic products, such as those derived from plastic, are often integrated into the building shell as well.

One challenge is the building's design. Does the appearance of the building really matter? If the pursuit of beauty, natural and human crafted, is important to creation care, what implications emerge for the design or redesign of the building shell? Another challenge is that myriad choices abound in relation to building materials. What variables are important if we are to be wise stewards? Water and energy resources are limited, and each locale has variables that affect water and energy efficiency. What needs to be considered if we are to make the best choices as environmental stewards?

In this chapter I will consider four primary issues related to creation care and the building shell: architectural design, material selection, water consumption and wastewater disposal, and energy efficiency. Each of these areas will be addressed with references to solutions that our ten featured congregations pursued, illustrating thoughtful stewardship in action.

ARCHITECTURAL DESIGN FOR BEAUTY

People of faith generally affirm that God is the source of beauty. The diverse forms of life in the world, contours of land and sea, and daytime and nighttime vistas are examples of beauty we attribute to the Creator. Apparently God values and delights in beauty. The beauty that surrounds us inspires us and brings us joy. Humanity is created in the image of God. We possess the capacity to recognize beauty. We possess the creative imagination to produce what is beautiful. When we create artifacts that are beautiful, we bear witness to the significance of beauty and reflect the very presence of God.

A faith community's values will be communicated through the design of its building shell. God demonstrated a commitment to beauty in guiding the design of both the tabernacle and the temple of ancient Israel. We have the opportunity to follow God's approach. When beauty is reflected in the building shell design, then faith affirmations about beauty take material form. The power of beauty—to delight, inspire, and bring joy—will be unleashed. The beauty of a building shell design is a creation care issue in that our creations are located in a natural world saturated with beauty, and our structures have the potential to add to the myriad expressions of beauty. Pursuit of beauty in building design demonstrates a commitment to preserving and perpetuating beauty in God's world.

I have intentionally avoided defining beauty. The perception of beauty involves intuition and taste. It is affected by exposure to and knowledge about artistic expressions across time and cultures. Identifying beauty varies from person to person, community to community, and epoch to epoch. I do not believe that there is any one ideal style of building shell design for faith communities. The history of synagogue and church design demonstrates that a host of expressions reflecting dimensions of beauty are possible and that, ultimately, determining whether something is beautiful depends on the impressions of multiple generations over a long period of time. While we cannot know whether our designs will withstand such scrutiny, we can do our best to make inspiring design choices today.

In any culture dominated by pragmatism, there is pressure to emphasize utility over beauty. Yielding to this temptation in building design can effectively, even if unintentionally, deny the significance of visual and material beauty. While the pursuit of beauty may not enhance the utilitarian function of the building shell per se, it does connect us to God's intentions for creation and enhance human existence. No singular formula for achieving beauty exists. Each community must determine the most appropriate expression for its particular setting and available resources.

For your congregation to cultivate beauty through building shell design and the interior environment, please consider the following suggestions:

- Engage the services of a registered architect. You will benefit from a professional's theoretical and practical training and have a seasoned guide as you work toward attaining a design of beauty.
- Enlist the help of visual artists in your faith community. Through their training and experience, they can help sensitize the community to beauty and discern what is best for your context.

- Consider the services of a liturgical consultant. A liturgical consultant works with congregations in exploring and designing the optimal environment for worship and ministry activities. They are especially aware of the history, theology, and range of designs associated with religious spaces.
- Explore the historical designs, symbols, and colors associated with art and architecture in your religious tradition. We are not limited by our past but may find real sources for creativity in the expressions of those who have gone before us. We may also discover ways of energizing familiar designs, provide continuity for believers across generations, and share in a recognizable visual lexicon in the built urban landscape.
- Maximize access to natural views. Glazed surfaces (whether they are windows, doors, skylights, or entire walls) provide opportunities to enjoy the beauty of the natural world. Providing access to natural views for the largest number of building occupants underscores our connection to the creation and is even rewarded by building rating systems such as LEED.
- Accentuate the beauty of natural materials. The innate beauty of materials such as wood and stone can be incorporated into designs in ways that maximize their appealing qualities.
- Be willing to invest creativity and financial resources in your building. God instructed the Israelites to bring their very best artistic talents and offerings to religious building. Allow those who are gifted with artistic imagination and skill to bear witness to the blessing God would share through them.

Beauty has been expressed in a number of ways among the congregations examined in this book. Keystone Community Church has used an attractive contemporary design featuring different shades of brick, metal supports, and curtain glass walls. The building, set along a tree line, becomes an inviting destination. The limestone façade of St. Gabriel Church exposes ancient embedded fossils, a reference to both creation in general and the specific geological history of the region. The primary entrance, made of oak and etched glass, is an expression of natural beauty. A glass curtain wall in its primary worship space provides visual access to the garden adjacent to it, and a spectrum of changing colors wash across its concrete surfaces through colored glass in the ceiling that filters natural light. Congregation Beth David has a low-profile design punctuated with Southwestern accents, complementing the California coastal terrain and nearby foothills. A trellis over the primary entrance, sculpted in a design to recall hands extending the ancient priestly blessing over the congregation (Num. 6:24–27), welcomes all who enter. Jewish Reconstructionist Congregation exhibits an iconic two-story ceremonial entry made of reclaimed maple and white limestone tiles from Israel. Its exterior is clad in reclaimed cypress, exhibiting a rich, warm façade. The glazing of the building provides a lively visual counterpoint and maximizes views of the natural world.

Holy Wisdom Monastery chose an inviting contemporary design, including a bell tower that features the bells from the previous building. Access to natural views is available from 99.5 percent of interior spaces. Eldridge Street Synagogue incorporates a variety of features associated with historical styles, including Gothic, Romanesque, and Moorish. Its recent restoration has renewed the beauty of its complex natural stone façade, stained glass windows, and seven roof finials. Unity Temple preserves the unique prairie-style design of Frank Lloyd Wright. The concrete surface of the exterior is punctuated with art glass windows and columns minimally decorated with geometric patterns. Varied horizontal and vertical surfaces, some of which are planters, bring energy and richness to the design.

The primary entrance and exterior façade of Jewish Reconstructionist Congregation. The two-story ceremonial entrance door of maple is featured here with its surrounding limestone tile arch. The primary entry door is located immediately to the left of the maple door (under the arch). Drought-resistant plantings and low gabion walls of reclaimed materials can be seen in the foreground along the sidewalk. (Author photo.)

BUILDING MATERIALS SELECTION

Selection of materials for a building is an important way to pursue creation care by providing congregations opportunities to repurpose existing materials, process recyclable content, utilize renewable natural resources, and reduce the landfill waste associated with construction projects. Accompanying benefits include reducing energy and emission of greenhouse gases associated with producing new materials. Using building materials produced closer to a building site is environmentally friendly too. The closer a manufacturer is to the project, the less fuel is needed to transport the materials. The local or regional economy also realizes collateral benefits through this choice.

A fundamental strategy for sustainable building is to reuse materials. We can adapt an existing building or select materials that have been collected and processed for reuse. Sometimes existing buildings can be renovated in ways that allow them to fulfill the existing and anticipated needs of a community. Distinctive architectural designs and excellence in craftsmanship may be retained and restored through this avenue. The restoration of Eldridge Street Synagogue, a historic building, is an example of this form of reuse. The beauty of the original building and furnishings and the unique heritage of the faith community were maintained while reusing existing durable materials and integrating recycled materials. The original stone and brick have been restored. Up to 85 percent of the original stained glass was retained, as was 95 percent of the wood. Nearly all of the original brass fixtures were salvaged as well. Reuse of durable materials can extend the lifespan of an existing building, allowing its beauty to be enjoyed for additional generations.

Reclaiming an idle building by a faith community can be an act of creation care and a catalyst for renewing a neighborhood, and it can be an effective way of limiting the materials and energy needed for a project. Site preparation costs (including earth movement, development of roadways or walkways, utility connections, and landscaping) can be minimized through using an existing structure. A general evaluation of the existing building would need to be done to assess the condition of the structure, materials, and systems (such as plumbing, electrical, heating, cooling, and ventilation). Structural defects, deteriorated or toxic materials, and faulty systems would need to be addressed.

Eldridge Street Synagogue and Museum at Eldridge Street's restored exterior façade. The unique architectural elements, including horseshoe arches and finials, have been carefully restored. A majority of the original stone, brick, and glass have been retained, an affirmation of the durability of the materials. (Photo © Kate Milford, courtesy of the Museum at Eldridge Street; used with permission.)

Compliance with present building codes (including the Americans with Disabilities Act, or ADA)[1] would need to be achieved as well. Challenges may include expressing the congregation's particular aesthetic of beauty or its religious identity, as when structures originally used for commercial space are adapted. But faith communities have used a variety of building styles throughout history.

An example of adapting an existing building is found at Grace Place, Chicago, Illinois. Grace Place houses an Episcopal congregation and center for community ministries (parish driven, ecumenical, and interreligious). Grace Episcopal Church, established in 1851, sought to retain its historic commitment to ministering to those in the city. They chose to reclaim a late nineteenth-century arts and crafts style commercial building in the Printers Row neighborhood of downtown Chicago on Dearborn Street. The building was added to the National Register of Historic Places in 1976 and has been designated a Chicago landmark. The renovation was completed in 1985. The wooden beam-and-post construction of the original structure was preserved in renovating its three stories and basement. The first and third floors and basement provide office and meeting spaces for a variety of religious and social groups. The second floor features an award-winning worship space designed by the architectural firm of Booth Hansen, Chicago. A curved, non-load-bearing interior wall with multiple openings for natural light and movement creates a sense of intimate space. Furnishings from the previous church building, including the baptismal font and wooden pews, have been incorporated into the new space. Open space rises above the altar, penetrating the floor above to the roof, creating a sense of transcendence. In 1989 the excellence of the interior design of the worship space was recognized with an award from the Chicago chapter of the American Institute of Architects. Adapting an existing building can be a profound way to recycle building materials and contribute to community renewal.

If the investments associated with retooling an existing building do not make good social or economic sense, it is possible to deconstruct an existing building and reuse its materials for a new project. A faith community may also acquire previously used materials such as brick, stone, lumber, glass, metalwork, doors, and lighting fixtures. Reusing materials can reduce the consumption of new resources, minimize landfill waste, create additional market value for existing materials, and create job opportunities related to the reclamation process. A network of people and resources connected to this emerging industry can be found through the Building Materials Reuse Association (BMRA; www.bmra.

org). The BMRA is a not-for-profit educational organization that shares information about the value of utilizing recycled building materials and assists the new industry's development. Habitat for Humanity has entered this field as well with the establishment of ReStores (see www.habitat.org/restores). The ReStores buy and sell used building materials in addition to donated new materials. Congregations could contribute to the recycling of building materials by deconstructing existing facilities in ways that preserve reusable materials or incorporate used materials in new projects.

New building products that utilize recycled waste are available as well. Concrete that contains fly ash is being produced for foundations, walkways, and other applications. Fly ash is a byproduct of coal when it is burned to generate electricity and also comes from furnaces used to make steel. Adding fly ash to concrete has been found to enhance its performance, making it more durable and resistant to deterioration from exposure to chemicals. Wood fiber, paper, plastic, steel, aluminum, and glass are being used to generate new building materials. Building shell products that are manufactured today with recycled materials include roofing material, engineered wood products, steel studs, lumber substitutes from plastics, framing connectors, nails, sheathing (material attached to roof and wall supports to provide a weatherproof exterior), siding (material attached over the wall sheathing), fascia (the material placed horizontally across the rafter ends on the outside of a building), soffit (the material used to cover the underneath surface of the roof overhang—adjacent to the fascia), windows, sewer pipes, gypsum board and plaster (used for interior wall and ceiling surfaces), trim (decorative material used as an accent on wall surfaces, often found along the base of a wall), and underlayment (material that lies between the subfloor and flooring material).

Reuse and Recycling at JRC

Jewish Reconstructionist Congregation (JRC) found multiple ways to use sustainable building materials. JRC found it cost effective to demolish their previous building. Some of the demolished building was salvaged, and suitable materials were repurposed. The concrete, concrete block, and brick of the old building was crushed and used as engineered fill. The old basement received this fill and was used as a base for the foundation of the new building. By using the previous building in this way, 96 percent of the material (2,700 tons) was diverted from a landfill. Broken masonry material from a nearby brickyard and nearby demolition projects was recycled for use in gabion walls (walls made by assembling metal cages filled with rubble) located along the perimeter of the property. Additional material was diverted from landfill in this way as well. The ceremonial entry and door to the synagogue was made of reclaimed maple from trees on the building site. Fifty percent of the wood used in the project was reused or Forest Stewardship Council certified, including recycled reclaimed cypress (incorporated into the exterior siding, day chapel, and main sanctuary) and walnut. Recycled glass was used in the building's insulation material. A large portion of recycled steel was incorporated into all steel products in the structure, including beams, columns, and studs. Fly ash was used in the polished concrete for the flooring of three levels. Forty-seven percent of all materials used for the new building were made within five hundred miles of the site.

Keystone Community Church used building materials with recycled content and brick and concrete from local manufacturers. Interior precast panels in their new building can be reused for future applications ("cradle to cradle" thinking). Polished, stained concrete is used as a flooring material for multiple reasons. No adhesives are required, it provides a low maintenance surface, and it retains and releases heat from the sun. St. Gabriel Church used concrete and steel products with recycled material content. Congregation Beth David used straw bales, a rapidly renewable material, on its two coldest walls. Recycled newsprint is incorporated into their building insulation as well. Pulaski Heights United Methodist Church used materials with recycled content, certified materials, and locally and regionally produced materials for its addition. Recycled materials were also incorporated into the Eldridge Street project. Insulation for the building contains material from recycled blue jeans; bathroom counters and stall dividers for basement facilities contain recycled plastic milk jugs; and fly ash was used in some of the new concrete.

Product labels should identify the recycled content. The Federal Trade Commission has issued guidelines for standardizing the use of environmental marketing. The origin of the recycled content may be identified as preconsumer or postconsumer material. Preconsumer materials are removed from the waste stream during the manufacturing process; postconsumer materials are discarded waste from household, commercial, and industrial sources. Certification programs mentioned in chapter 3 can help identify potential products and verify the claims of manufacturers. LEED material guides and documentation from the websites of manufacturers can provide guidance as well.[2]

Assistance with selecting creation-care-oriented new building materials is available by using the product certification systems noted in chapter 3. The Forest Stewardship Council, Scientific Certification Systems, Green Seal, and Cradle to Cradle programs were mentioned as examples. As a congregation assesses its needs for building products, in consultation with building professionals, it can make a commitment to supporting manufacturers and suppliers that value environmental stewardship. Certified products use renewable resources, minimize energy costs for production, and release minimal toxic contamination. When selecting certified products, a congregation can give priority to local or regional suppliers, thus treasuring the area's natural resources, minimizing transportation costs for materials, and contributing to the economic viability of the immediate community. It is important for a congregation to communicate to all parties involved in the building project that use of certified materials is a priority.

Reuse and Recycling at Holy Wisdom Monastery

Holy Wisdom Monastery also chose to deconstruct an existing building, Benedict House, on its site. Some items such as the organ and walk-in cooler were refurbished and installed in the new building. Nine tons of building material was recovered from the deconstruction of the original structure and donated to Habitat ReStore. Just over 8,628 tons of material was recycled, including concrete that was crushed and used as a base for parking areas and drives and even sculpted into berms around the property. Only 12.5 tons was sent to a landfill. In all, 99.75 percent of the previous building was diverted from waste disposal as landfill. Reused materials accounted for 12.5 percent of the total material costs for the project. Materials with recycled content constituted 21 percent of the material costs. Ten percent of the building material costs were for rapidly renewable resources (primarily bamboo for flooring and ceiling applications, and agrifiber board for cases and cabinets). Nearly 60 percent of all wood was Forest Stewardship Council certified. And 28 percent of material costs were associated with local or regional sources.

WATER USE EFFICIENCY AND GREYWATER RECYCLING

Water is essential for all life. Factors such as rainfall patterns, population growth, and pollution affect the availability of clean water. According to UN-Water, a program of the United Nations, 97.5 percent of the earth's water is saltwater.[3] Only 2.5 percent of all water is freshwater. Of that 2.5 percent, ice and snow account for 70 percent of the total volume (in mountainous regions, Antarctica, and the Arctic region), 30 percent is located in underground sources, and only 0.3 percent is present in freshwater lakes and rivers.[4] Freshwater is used for irrigation, industry, and households. Freshwater consumption is growing at a rate faster than the population. By 2025 water usage is projected to increase by 50 percent in the developing world and by 18 percent in developed countries.[5] An important dimension of creation care is to maximize the availability of clean water. The building shell can be developed in ways that use water responsibly.

A primary focus of water use for congregations is conservation. Limiting the amount of water we use can help ensure adequate supplies of water for our communities. Plumbing fixtures that minimize the use of water can contribute to water efficiency. Low-flow devices are available for faucets, showerheads, and toilets. Conventional faucet aerators do not compensate for changes in water pressure when activated, so the greater the water pressure, the more water is used. Low-flow aerators regulate the water pressure so that the same volume of water flows from the faucet even as the pressure changes. Low-flow showerheads incorporate a similar regulating aerator and can include multiple flow settings. Water use can be lowered by as much as 40 percent with installation of these aerators, generally reducing water use from about four gallons per minute to about two and one-half gallons per minute or less.[6]

Toilets present another opportunity for water conservation. Standard toilets can use up to 3.5 gallons per flush. Low-flow toilets use a maximum of 1.6 gallons per flush. Some high-efficiency toilet models are driving the amount of water necessary for flushing even lower. Federal regulations have mandated the use of low-flow toilets in new construction projects since 1994 in an effort to assist with water conservation efforts, but standard toilets are still being used in many places. Since 1980 dual-flush toilet technology has been available. Dual-flush toilets today use about 0.8 gallons of water for liquid waste and 1.6 gallons for solid waste. Use of low-flow plumbing fixtures will help the congregation realize significant water conservation. Waterless urinals are an important water-saving alternative to consider as well. Because these urinals require no water, they need no water piping, flush valves, or other control hardware, reducing maintenance of the units. The bowl of the unit contains a chemical that has a lighter specific gravity than urine and therefore floats on top of the waste material. The urine is effectively pushed into the drain, and the chemical forms a barrier that prevents sewer odor from escaping into the restroom. The chemical is present in the bowl, so no flushing or handle is required to initiate waste disposal. The chemical does need to be renewed regularly, but little additional maintenance is needed. With the increasing use of waterless urinals in public areas, the technology is growing in familiarity and product efficiency continues to develop.

St. Gabriel Church and Holy Wisdom Monastery use a combination of low-flow water fixtures, dual-flush toilets, and waterless urinals in their buildings. The low-flow hand sink fixtures in the restrooms of Holy Wisdom Monastery even have small photovoltaic cells to minimize the energy needed to trigger the sensor that turns the faucets on and off. The Holy Wisdom community is achieving a 43.7 percent decrease in indoor water usage over that of a conventional building. Jewish Reconstructionist Congregation uses low-flow water fixtures and dual-flush toilets and expects to reduce its water usage by 40 percent over conventional fixtures. Keystone Community Church and Pulaski Heights Church use low-flow water fixtures and waterless urinals. Pulaski Heights is testing the waterless urinal technology with one fixture before changing existing urinals. Congregation Beth David and Temple Emanuel use low-flow water fixtures.

Wastewater produced by occupants of a building is identified as either greywater or blackwater. Greywater is wastewater from sinks, showers, and laundry. Blackwater is wastewater that may contain human feces, urine, or food debris. Greywater can be recovered and reused for select applications, such as to irrigate plantings or to flush toilets. Greywater reuse does require some filtration in order to meet building code requirements, for it does contain a certain amount of bacteria. Commercial greywater treatment systems are available that use natural treatment (for example, plants or microorganisms and bacteria) or mechanical filtration. Reclamation and reuse of greywater will increase congregational water efficiency and reduce the quantity of wastewater that requires processing by municipal systems.

ENERGY EFFICIENCY

Energy efficiency can be achieved in multiple ways in building projects. Orienting a building on a site to maximize daylight in the building can help reduce the need for interior lights. Buildings can also be oriented in ways that take advantage of potential solar energy and prevailing wind conditions. In general, orienting a building in North America along an east-west access to maximize a southern exposure will increase the potential for using daylight for illumination and assist with temperature control (heating and cooling).[7] A method for controlling sun exposure throughout the day on south-facing glass surfaces will be needed. Differing latitudes and site conditions influence the particular design options for a building. Colder climates have different needs from warmer climates. Combinations of natural site features, landscaping, overhangs, and window coverings can be used to attain the most advantageous levels of sun exposure. To maximize the use of prevailing winds for natural ventilation, buildings can be oriented perpendicularly to the winds. Operable windows, fans, and openings can be incorporated to reduce heating and cooling costs. Each building site has unique geographical and environmental conditions that will affect building orientation. Architects have software programs that can reproduce the variables of a particular location and site and make specific recommendations for a project.

Passive designs decrease the need for mechanical systems to provide thermal comfort, a method that helps to reduce the energy a building consumes. Building materials naturally absorb solar energy. Water, concrete, brick, walls made of earth (for example, rammed earth or compressed earth blocks), and sandstone have a high capacity for storing solar energy. For heating, the solar energy is directed toward the materials in ways that maximize its storage so that the energy can be radiated into the interior building space. Concrete walls and floors can be designed in this way. Trombe or solar walls can also be created. A Trombe wall can be made of materials such as concrete, compressed earth, or water tanks. The wall is oriented to maximize sun exposure. The wall has a glazed surface on the outside with a space for air flow between the glazing and wall. Vents are located at the top and bottom of the wall to allow for natural air flow. Stored heat from the wall is released into the building at night via this design. For cooling, a building can be designed to reflect solar energy, or shading systems can be developed (through landscaping or artificial shades or both). Glazed surfaces, such as windows, skylights, and reflective exterior and interior surfaces can be designed to contribute to the heating and cooling needs of the building.

Other aspects of the building shell can be constructed in ways that maximize energy efficiency. A foundation can be insulated in new construction projects. A vapor retarder (or vapor diffusion retarder) can be installed to help control moisture or exposure to other harmful vapors in basements, in crawl spaces, or through slab-on-grade foundations. Limiting moisture helps to maintain a comfortable level of humidity in a building; reduce potential moisture damage, such as deterioration of materials or the growth of molds; and enhance interior air quality.

Exterior walls can be insulated with material appropriate for the climate of the site. Insulation material is labeled with an R-value, which measures the ability of the product to impede heat flow through it. The higher the R-value of the product, the more effective its insulating property. Different climatic conditions require different R-values. The US Department of Energy has a website (Insulation Fact Sheet, www.ornl.gov/sci/roofs+walls/insulation) through its Oak Ridge National Laboratory that can give you an idea of what level of R-value is needed for your geographical region. Recycled paper and glass is used in some insulation materials today. For example, recycled newspaper or other postconsumer paper can be used to manufacture cellulose insulation. Recycled paper and glass can be used to make fiberglass insulation. And rapidly renewable resources such as straw bales can be used for insulation. A building wrap can also be applied. A building wrap is an air barrier and vapor retarder that helps to control the level of moisture that enters through the exterior walls and can help to control air infiltration in a building. Limiting the amount of air infiltration through the walls can assist in regulating the interior air temperature, which makes the heating and cooling systems more energy efficient.

St. Gabriel Church uses the maximum insulation recommended for its building. The concrete walls and floor store and release thermal energy, providing passive solar heating as a supplement to the mechanical heating system. Congregation Beth David designed a tight building shell to maximize energy efficiency. They used R-35-rated straw bales on the two coldest walls (north and east), two-by-six-inch stud framing with R-21 wall insulation, and R-54 ceiling insulation (a combination of R-38 cellulose and R-16 rigid Insulam, a wood-reinforced, plastic-composite product) in their sanctuary. Solar heat is harnessed through the concrete masonry walls, straw bale walls with extra plaster, and eleven water tanks, as well as two Trombe walls on the south side of the building. Jewish Reconstructionist Congregation used six inches of fiberglass insulation, manufactured with recycled glass jars, in its walls and roof. The Eldridge Street project greatly improved the minimal insulation of its historic building.

Openings in the building shell can provide natural light for interior space. The shell itself can be oriented in a way that maximizes the harvesting of natural daylight. Windows, clerestory windows (located in an exterior wall that rises above an adjoining roof), skylights, and light conveyors (tubes that channel light from a roof to an interior space) can be located strategically throughout the shell to maximize harvesting seasonal daylight levels. Light shelves, which are highly reflective horizontal overhangs adjacent to windows, can also be placed on the interior or exterior of a building. The shelves can redirect natural light deeper into an interior space and also provide shading. Computer modeling can be done today that simulates the usual amount of seasonal light in a given location to optimize building orientation and fenestration for daylighting and to reduce dependency on artificial light.

Openings for daylighting can also cause heat loss and gain. A single pane of clear glass has an R-value of 1, and a double pane of clear glass, an R-value of 2. Special coatings are available for glass or glazed surfaces today. Low-emissivity (Low-E) coatings, which are nearly invisible metal or metallic oxide layers deposited on the surface of glass, can be applied to help control heat transfer. Glass treated in this way is a little more expensive than noncoated glass but can reduce energy loss by 30 to 50 percent.[8] The R-value of a window can be increased if the window is double glazed, which means that there is air space between two panes of glass. The insulation value increases if there is more than one air space between glass panes (as in three panes of glass, or triple glazing). Replacing the air between the panes of glass with argon gas will enhance the R-value even more. Insulated frames or those made of low-conductivity material will also increase R-value.

Congregation Beth David is designed so that every room in the building, toilets excluded, needs only natural light during the day. The building has one hundred and ninety-four windows, including thirty-eight clerestory windows, ten skylights, eight interior windows, twenty door transoms, and twenty-one solar tubes. An architectural lantern above the sanctuary bimah provides clerestory lighting, and a plenum (air chamber) allows cool air to enter at night and warm air to escape during the day in the summer. Light shelves are used on all south walls. The shelves serve to shield water tanks from the intense noon sun in the summer and to reflect the low winter sun deeper into the building.

View of interior courtyard at Congregation Beth David, with windows on multiple levels and solar panels. The building is shaped like a bagel, with the courtyard the open area in the center. This shape provides space for outdoor events and protects participants from the wind. Clerestory windows can be seen just above the solar panels on the roof. An exterior light shelf can be seen beneath the middle row of windows, providing a reflective surface for light to enter windows above and a shade for windows below. Lights shelves are installed on all south-facing windows. (Photo provided by Congregation Beth David; used with permission.)

Jewish Reconstructionist Congregation uses windows, solar light tubes, and clerestory windows with light shelves for daylighting. Ninety percent of the building receives natural light. The Low-E glass windows are insulated and gas filled. Holy Wisdom Monastery uses windows, solar light tubes, and clerestory windows to provide daylight to 85 percent of its interior spaces. They also used Low-E glass windows that are insulated and gas filled.

Unity Temple exhibits many windows, clerestory windows, and skylights to harvest daylight. Low-E glass has been installed in the kitchen and in some classrooms to increase energy efficiency.

Insulation, a radiant barrier, and cool roofing systems can increase the energy efficiency of roofs. Insulation is placed under the roof to help stabilize the interior temperature. Radiant barriers are made of a material that efficiently reflects radiant heat and reduces summer heat gain and winter heat loss. Radiant barriers are especially effective in hot climates, reducing the radiant heat that enters an attic space. Radiant barriers come in various forms: reflective foil, reflective metal roof shingles (the barrier is on the underside of the shingles), reflective laminated roof sheathing, or even reflective chips that can be applied over loose-fill insulation.

A cool roofing system uses materials that minimize the amount of heat transferred to the building below it. The materials used in the system reflect much of the incoming solar radiation and quickly dissipate the heat that is retained by the roofing materials, a process called thermal emittance. The combination of these effects minimizes the solar radiation that penetrates the building. Use of cool roofing systems can improve the comfort level of a building's interior by reducing the amount of heat transfer. During the warm season, the interior of the building stays cooler, which reduces energy costs and extends the life of the air-conditioning equipment. The reduction in heat through the roof extends the life of the roofing materials as well, lowering overall maintenance and replacement costs.

Cool roofing systems can combat the energy phenomenon of "heat island effect" mentioned in chapter 5. Such systems increase air quality, reduce energy demands, and save money. The US Department of Energy has developed a Cool Roof Calculator through its Oak Ridge Laboratory (http://www.ornl.gov/sci/roofs+walls/facts/CoolCalcEnergy.htm) to help people estimate the cooling and heating savings for their facilities. The US Environmental Protection Agency's Energy Star Program website also provides cool roofing information and identifies products.

Green or vegetative roofs are an attractive alternative for extending creation care. A green roof is a prepared flat or sloped roof surface planted with vegetation. A green roof has multiple layers, usually including a roof deck (base), a water- and root-resistant membrane, insulation, a filter layer that contains soil, and a layer of plants. Engineered soil is used for green roofs to provide a more lightweight, well-draining planting medium. Green roofs can be categorized as *extensive* or *intensive*. *Extensive roofs* use lighter-weight plants such as grasses, sedum (a family of succulent plants, also called stonecrop or orpine), or other ground covers. Less soil is needed to maintain these low-lying plants. *Intensive green roofs* are planted with larger vegetation, such as shrubs or trees. Additional structural support in a building and deeper soil are needed to support intensive roof plantings. The needed structural support is based on the potential weight of the vegetation and soil fully saturated with water. Green roofs can be designed for new construction projects or developed for renovated buildings.

Green roofs have multiple benefits for the community. The plantings can effectively capture and process rainwater runoff (storm-water management), as noted in chapter 5. Green roofs can absorb water, direct excess runoff to appropriate collection systems, and provide initial filtration of the water, which improves runoff water quality. The roof temperature is reduced with the use of a green roof. Heat island effect can be reduced in this way, and the building's interior temperature can be stabilized. A green roof provides additional insulation and protects the roofing system from the effects of direct sunlight and extreme temperatures. Finally, green roofs provide natural habitats for wildlife and have aesthetic appeal.

Green roofs are not maintenance free. Initial plantings will require attention as they become established, and ongoing checks are important as with all landscape installations. Extensive green roofs require less attention, especially if they are planted with drought-resistant plants. Periodic checks to control weeds, disease, and spurious tree seedlings are necessary. Engineered soil is usually devoid of the weed seeds found in regular topsoil, enhancing weed control. Supplemental water needs, if required, can be addressed through a drip irrigation system using recycled rainwater runoff to deliver small amounts of water to the roots of the plants, minimizing evaporation during watering.

St. Gabriel Church uses roof insulation and a reflective material on its roof to maximize energy efficiency. Jewish Reconstructionist Congregation uses roof insulation, a white reflective material on its roof, and reflective paving to reduce heat island effect in its neighborhood. Holy Wisdom Monastery uses a combination of roof insulation, white reflective roof material, vegetation on two roof surfaces, and reflective pavers on walkways to assist with minimizing energy demands. Annunciation Byzantine Catholic Church is anticipating a green roof on a portion of its facility. Permeable pavement and intentional landscape design also contribute to reducing heat island effect in their area.

ALTERNATIVE ENERGY SYSTEMS AND COGENERATION

Today congregations can choose from a range of options to supplement energy sources such as nuclear power, coal, and natural gas. The first is the Green Power Network, which is expanding across the United States.[9] Utility companies are gradually investing in alternative energy sources such as solar, wind, biomass, and landfill gas systems. Costs associated with producing energy from renewable sources are a little higher than conventional sources, so utility companies have created programs that allow customers to subscribe to green energy sources by paying a small premium for each kilowatt they use. The utility company then uses the premium to support new renewable-energy development. The higher the number of subscribers to the program, the less dependent the utility is on conventional energy sources. Use of green power reduces the carbon footprint of a congregation, promotes the development of renewable energy, and models creation care potential to the immediate and wider community. St. Gabriel Church, Jewish Reconstructionist Congregation, Holy Wisdom Monastery, and Temple Emmanuel all purchase green energy from their local utility companies.

While a congregation probably cannot completely rely on alternative energy for all of its needs, solar, wind, and ground source (or geothermal) systems are increasingly viable sources for energy. Solar energy can be harnessed for heating space, as mentioned above in the discussion of energy efficiency. Solar energy can also be used for heating water and producing electricity. Solar water heating systems consist of solar collectors and well-insulated storage tanks. They use either a passive or an active system design. Passive systems rely on gravity to move water heated by the sun from the solar collector to the storage tank. Active systems use a pump and controls to circulate fluid. Passive systems are usually less expensive than active systems but may not be as efficient. Different active solar water-heating systems are designed for varying climates. Direct circulation systems can circulate water through collectors and into the storage tank. Indirect circulation systems can circulate a nonfreezing heat-transfer fluid through collectors and then through a heat exchanger in the storage tank to heat water. One or two storage tanks may used in a system. In a two-tank system, water is preheated with the solar collector before moving to the conventional backup water heater. In one-tank systems, a supplemental heater is added to the water storage tank. Solar hot-water systems usually require supplemental energy for heating water on cloudy days or when demand is high. The costs of solar hot-water systems have fallen in the past fifteen years as the technology associated with them has improved and as they have become more commonplace. Financial incentives to reduce the upfront costs of these systems are available in some areas. Check government websites, manufacturers, and with local utility companies for possible incentives.

Harnessing solar energy is a viable option for supplementing energy for a congregation's building. A solar energy system can include solar cells (or photovoltaic cells), battery storage, and an inverter for electrical current. Solar cells translate natural sunlight into electricity in the form of direct current (DC, the kind of current in a car battery). The cells are usually wired together into modules to produce a photovoltaic array. Arrays are often mounted on a roof or ground surface. The array produces the direct current, which can be used as it is generated or stored in one or more batteries. To use the energy from the solar cells or batteries, electricity must be inverted from DC current to alternating current (AC, the type of current we get through our wall-mounted electrical outlets).

Solar cells are manufactured in a variety of forms today. They continue to be produced for commercial application in panels, as they have been since the 1970s (although for much less money), but they are also being embedded in thinner and more flexible materials. Research into embedding them in various building materials is also being conducted. Solar cells will probably not meet all of our energy needs, at least not in the near future. Their efficiency at translating light into energy is limited, and they depend on the availability of sunlight. Different latitudes, seasonal changes, and cloud patterns affect the presence and strength of sunlight. An analysis of one's geographical area needs to be done to determine the sunlight potential and feasibility of harnessing solar energy. But real potential for including solar cells in our buildings exists, and as with solar heating, financial assistance for renewable energy initiatives is available.

Glass, Beauty, and Creation Care

Architectural glass artist Sarah Hall is on the leading edge of creating commissions for faith communities featuring photovoltaic (solar cell) art glass.[10] Hall was trained in the field of architectural glass in the United Kingdom and Israel. She has been fulfilling commissions in North America and Europe since the 1980s, has published books about art glass, and has garnered multiple awards for her work.[11] Since 2002 she has been collaborating with solar energy specialists in Germany to integrate solar energy harvesting into her art glass. With a design studio in Canada and fabrication studio in Germany, Hall has achieved four installations with photovoltaic cells. Hall's 2007 project *True North/Lux Nova* ("New Light"), is the central element of a wind tower that provides natural ventilation for the new underground theology library at Regent College on the campus of the University of British Columbia, Vancouver. The glass column features colored and textured glass with twelve dichroic glass crosses that produce a wide range of colors. Lettering of the Lord's Prayer in Aramaic is woven throughout the panels. Solar cells are integrated into the installation to collect energy during the day and provide electricity to power a luminous column of blue, violet, and white light via a column of LEDs at night. The light sequence is controlled by a computer program and synchronized with a contemporary violin soundtrack by Oliver Schroer entitled "The Lord's Prayer." The cells themselves also provide texture and color for the overall design.

Hall's most recent solar commission is for Cathedral of the Holy Family, Saskatoon, Saskatchewan. This is the first new Catholic cathedral to be built in Canada in the last fifty years and is scheduled to be dedicated in May 2012. Three monumental south-facing windows entitled *Lux Gloria* ("Light of Glory") are composed of fifty-four panels of art glass embedded with 1,113 solar cells. The cells will generate energy for the congregation's needs and be channeled into the Saskatoon energy grid. Cathedral of the Holy Family is the first cathedral in the world to feature solar cells in its glass work.

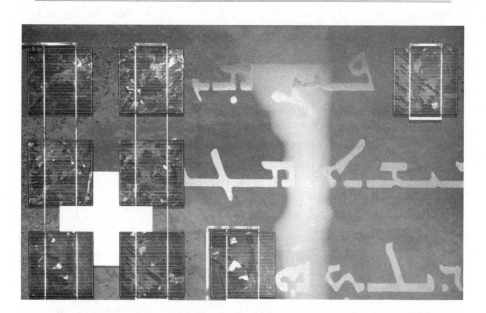

Detail of glass panel for *True North/Lux Nova* wind tower by Sarah Hall. A Greek cross, on the left, is positioned between solar cells that are linked together (four squares in the lower left corner with white wires running across and between them). On the right half of the photo, Aramaic writing is located between solar cells. Eight square cells can be seen in the photo. (Photo by Ken McAlister; used with permission.)

Congregation Beth David utilizes the sun's energy through its passive solar features, noted earlier in the chapter. They also use photovoltaic panels on their roof and generate 50 percent of their required electricity from this alternative energy source. A portion of the roof surface of Holy Wisdom monastery is covered by photovoltaic panels as well. At present they derive 13 percent of their electricity from these panels. Over time they would like to expand their solar generating capacity to cover 100 percent of their electrical needs.

Wind has been harnessed for hundreds of years through the use of windmills. Historically, it has been used to pump water or grind grain, but today turbines are being used to produce electricity as well. Wind turbines are set high above the ground to capture faster, less turbulent air movement. The blades of the turbine power a generator in the unit that produces electricity. Turbines can produce electricity for the immediate owner alone or can be tied into the utility grid in order to sell electricity back to the utility company. Being connected to the utility grid also provides a backup energy source. Automatic switching sends electricity to the utility if an excess supply is generated.

Wind energy systems use a renewable energy source and do not produce any greenhouse gases. They can provide energy for the congregation and even create revenue. Older turbines tended to generate an uncomfortable level of noise, but more recent designs have mostly eliminated this issue. Care should be taken to locate the turbines so that they pose the least threat to wildlife, such as birds or bats, that might collide with them. Wind patterns vary from one location to another, so an analysis of the potential for harnessing this renewable energy source will be necessary to determine if your congregation is a viable candidate to benefit from this power source. An average annual wind speed of at least nine miles per hour is needed to consider this option. The initial cost of a wind energy system can be substantial, but if a congregation is a good candidate for the system, the investment can be competitive with conventional energy sources when calculated over the lifespan of the system.[12] Wind energy systems are being designed today for multiple users as well, so it may be possible to work with your immediate neighbors in pursuing this supplemental energy source.

Ground source energy uses natural sources of heat inside the earth to produce electricity or heat. Harnessing steam or hot water from underground constitutes most geothermal power generation today. A direct-use system consists of a well drilled into a geothermal reservoir to provide a stream of hot water. A different method of ground source energy can be harnessed for congregational building heating and cooling needs. The earth holds a certain amount of heat due to exposure to the sun. Several feet below ground the temperature begins to maintain an average.[13] A ground source heat pump relies on the relatively constant temperature of the earth throughout the year, warmer than the air above it in the winter and cooler than the air above it in the summer. Depending on the latitude, the range is usually between 45° and 75°F. A ground source heat pump, a mechanical system of piping, heat exchanger, and controls are used to circulate water or other fluids through this layer of soil. The heat pump consists of a series of pipes buried underground in wells through which the fluid is circulated. The fluid flows in one of two directions depending on the need: to transfer heat from the ground to the building in the winter and to transfer heat from a building to the ground in the summer. Ground source systems can augment water heating as well, and heat pumps can be used in most parts of the United States.

Holy Wisdom Monastery incorporates a ground source system into its energy program. They have thirty-nine vertical wells that are each 300 feet deep. The field of wells is located beneath the parking area for the building. Congregations are also using ground source systems for historical restoration projects.[14] Trinity Church (1871), Boston, Massachusetts, initiated a deep well system in 2002. They had six wells drilled 45 to 75 feet apart to a depth of 1,500 feet each. The system is designed to heat and cool both the church (14,000 square feet) and the adjoining parish house (15,000 square feet).

Unity Temple Restoration Foundation has funded the design of a ground source heat pump HVAC system that is construction-ready. The building was originally fitted with a forced air system, but its inefficiency led to installing a steam system early in its history. Architectural Consulting Engineers, Chicago, has designed a system that reuses the building's original piping and ductwork.[15]

Since Unity Temple is a historic structure, care is taken to document the condition of everything before any alterations are made and to monitor conditions that may affect the integrity of the building. For several years the church has been using a single test well to gather initial data. The well is 300 feet and generates the heating and cooling for the clergy offices. Available land for drilling wells is quite limited, but some studies are showing that deep wells are particularly efficient. A proposal to drill nine deep wells (to 650 feet each) is being considered. Energy savings with ground source systems are impressive. Like other alternative energy systems they do have higher initial costs. Financial assistance for ground source systems is also available.

ADDRESSING THE BUILDING SHELL

The four primary issues related to building shell design that have been discussed—architectural design, material selection, water consumption and wastewater disposal, and energy efficiency—can all be addressed in new construction, renovation, and historical preservation projects. Beauty can also be achieved in any type of project, whether a new building or an existing one. Providing outdoor views maximizes exposure to the beauty of the creation. Existing features of historical buildings may limit exposure to external vistas (at least in some styles of building design or some portions of the interior space, such as the worship space). Stained or art glass installations usually exhibit an intrinsic beauty of their own, however, and add to the overall beauty of building design. The overall goal is to cultivate spaces that inspire visual delight and wonder.

Material selection affects all types of building projects. Varying opportunities will be available for reusing materials, using materials with levels of recycled content, or selecting materials from renewable sources. Historical projects may allow for a narrower range of materials at times, but they may also be excellent candidates for integrating previously used materials. Remember the value of life-cycle costing and using local and regional materials as well. All types of projects will be more environmentally sustainable when building materials can ultimately be reintegrated into the production stream at the end of their life and when the materials are drawn from the local economy.

Attending to water and energy use is an avenue for creation care in all building projects as well. Kitchens, restrooms, and bathing facilities with water-saving features can be designed for new or existing buildings. Greywater can be reused in some settings and is an option worth considering. Maximizing insulation and daylight harvesting and pursuing alternative energy sources can be considered for new, renovation, or historical projects. The primary challenge may be in securing knowledgeable assistance in design, materials, and construction that will be needed to achieve the desired stewardship goals.

CHAPTER 7

The Interior Environments in Which We Live

According to EPA statistics, most of us spend about 90 percent of our time inside buildings.[1] The quality of those interior spaces affects our health on multiple levels. Several factors need to be considered as faith communities seek to create and occupy environments in which to worship and minister to others. Beauty, indoor air quality, product selection, architectural features such as green walls, occupant comfort, lighting, and cleaning programs all have a part to play in designing creation care oriented interiors. Each will be examined below, with select examples from our ten congregations illustrating thoughtful choices.

ATTENTION TO BEAUTY

Beauty pertains to both interior environments and outside design. God's instructions for designing the interior of the tabernacle and temple included attention to beauty. The reasons and suggestions for pursuing beauty in exterior design noted in chapter 6 are important for excellent interior design as well. Natural expressions and materials combined with human creativity and imagination continue to provide avenues for unleashing beauty. Several examples of beauty in relation to interior design illustrate a broad range of possibilities.

Temple Emanuel bimah in the primary worship space. The banyan tree motif can be seen in the wooden branches radiating from the central ark to the ceiling. The tapestry around the ark, *ner tamid* (eternal flame), and short trunks for the reading desk and other objects build on this motif. The wall behind the bimah, composed of local stone, is visible as well. (Photo by Temple Emanuel; used with permission.)

Temple Emmanuel chose to highlight the beauty of the natural world in a more direct way through the interior design of its first sanctuary (mentioned in chapter 4). The design of the ark and bimah were inspired by the tropical banyan tree. The ark radiates branches to other trunks across the platform and to the ceiling. Replicated stumps hold the Torah scrolls in the ark. A colorful fiber tapestry featuring scripture passages represents the bark of the tree. A *ner tamid* (eternal flame), resembling a bird's nest, hovers over the ark. Short trunks serve to hold flower arrangements or other objects. Potted plants and medium-sized rocks are scattered across the bimah. The overall image evokes a tree of life. A large memorial wall serves as the backdrop to the bimah. The wall is made of locally quarried stone and serves as a reminder of the Western Wall in Jerusalem. The design and materials feature the beauty of nature in an imaginative, attractive, and focused way.

Jewish Reconstructionist Congregation has created attractive spaces for worship in its day chapel, on the first floor, and main sanctuary, on the third floor. The ceiling and walls of the day chapel are finished with reclaimed cypress. The wood is installed in an undulating pattern to give the room a tent-like feel, a reference perhaps to "How fair are your tents, O Jacob, Your dwellings, O Israel!" (Num. 24:5). The east wall of glass faces a rock garden and tall, vine-covered gabion wall. The ark is made from local fallen trees. The main sanctuary has an east wall of glass as well and looks out onto the tops of adjacent trees creating a powerful connection to the natural world. The interior space incorporates reclaimed cypress and walnut from local fallen trees. The ark for the Torah scrolls and the solar-powered *ner tamid* were designed by artist David Bachrach. Reclaimed and recycled materials of wood and metal are incorporated into the ark, and the quilted cloth lining for the ark was designed by textile artist Pamela Hill. Even the Early Childhood Center received commissioned art. An interactive mural designed by JRC member and artist Rebecca Hamlin occupies a primary wall and provides an inviting focal point for the center.

Unity Temple's interior exhibits careful attention to details in concert with Frank Lloyd Wright's prairie style. Distinctive rectilinear and geometric elements are incorporated into many features of the interior, including skylights, art glass windows, lighting fixtures, trim, and furniture. A color palette of lighter yellow, green, and brown tones reminiscent of the Midwestern prairie dominates the worship space. Oak is the primary wood used in the space. Its coloring provides a warm contrasting tone and was used for the organ grille, liturgical furniture, congregational seating, and trim. Oak strips are woven throughout the space to accent and unify the interior. With natural light filling the room through amber-colored skylight glass and clerestory, the overall effect is stunning.

Interior of primary worship space at Unity Temple. Wright's accent on the horizontal axis is present. Strong rectilinear, geometric patterns are found in the oak woodwork on the walls, ceiling, and in the light fixtures. The skylights (above) and clerestory art glass (above the congregational seating on the right side of the photo) exhibit Wright's geometric designs as well. (Author photo.)

The Eldridge Street Synagogue has preserved its original beauty and continues to enhance its interior space. The original painted and stenciled finishes on wall, column, and ceiling surfaces were cleaned and conserved but left to reflect the patina of time. In some places, paint that was lifting off the surface could be reattached. If an area had deteriorated to the point of no return, painting (and replastering, if needed) was done to match the surrounding surface. The flooring was sanded with steel wool and refinished while preserving the timeworn ruts in the boards, the wear left as a reminder of the devotion of previous generations. Sixty-seven original stained glass windows, containing more than 250 panels, and brass light fixtures were all cleaned and restored. The hand-carved walnut ark with original red velvet lining, bimah, lectern, menorah, and *ner tamid* were cleaned and, if needed, returned to their original locations. Both the beauty of the original artwork and the beauty of its devotional use were treasured in this project. The missing original stained glass rose window on the east elevation and lack of documentation concerning its initial design presented an opportunity to add a contemporary expression of beauty. The Museum at Eldridge Street commissioned a new window, which draws on historical imagery and complements existing mural designs. It features a central Star of David located in a field of blue. Smaller, yellow, five-pointed stars surround the central six-pointed star. An ongoing commitment to beauty is reflected in the synagogue.

INDOOR AIR QUALITY

Most of us spend a majority of the day in constructed spaces, whether in houses, factories, offices, stores, restaurants, motorized transport, schools, or places of worship. Achieving an optimal level of indoor air quality in a building is a challenge. The building shell can be built in such a way that little air is allowed to flow between the outside and inside spaces. Minimizing air transfer produces a "tight" building and aids with air heating and cooling efficiency by recirculating the same air, yielding lower energy costs. Sealed windows (windows that do not open) were introduced in the twentieth century by building designers, in part, to increase this efficiency. While prohibiting fresh air from entering the interior space increases energy efficiency, it can also contribute to poor air quality. Recirculated air will diminish in quality over time. Oxygen is inhaled by the building occupants and carbon dioxide is exhaled, and over time the carbon dioxide level can become unhealthy. Allowing the building shell to admit fresh air can improve interior air quality by renewing the oxygen level and reducing the carbon dioxide level. Monitoring the carbon dioxide levels in a building can assist with maintaining a healthy quality of air.

Interior temperature and humidity are also affected by the introduction of fresh air. Air outside a building may be a different temperature and humidity from that within a building. Introducing fresh air can heat up or cool off the interior environment and alter the humidity and thus affect the comfort of the occupants.

Passive (nonmechanical) and active (mechanical) ventilation systems are designed to address interior air quality, including temperature and humidity. Passive ventilation capitalizes on the presence of natural air movement and the thermal properties of air. The orientation of a building on the site may be adjusted to take advantage of prevailing wind patterns in a particular area (noted in chapter 6). Operable windows and vents can be installed to allow for transfer of air. Warm air rises naturally and can be harnessed by locating vents near the bottom of the building to allow cooler fresh air to enter and near the top to allow warmer interior air to escape. Windows and vents can be either mechanically controlled or designed so that occupants can adjust them. Control systems that use computer and sensor technology to automatically open and close windows and vents can maximize the benefits of natural air movement.

Holy Wisdom Monastery interior of primary worship space. Strategically placed clear glass maximizes natural light in the worship space. Multiple windows can be manually operated to facilitate natural passive ventilation. The flooring is made of bamboo, a rapid-growing renewable wood source. (Author photo.)

An active system depends on mechanical devices to control air movement and monitor air quality. HVAC is the industry shorthand for a mechanical heating, ventilation, and air-conditioning system. Equipment for the HVAC system of a congregation may include a furnace (using forced air) or boiler (using water) to provide heat, a central air conditioner to provide cooling, or an electric air-source or ground-source heat pump to provide both heating and cooling in a single integrated system. Forced-air systems use ductwork (sheet metal or flexible tube material) to move the air; water systems use pipes and radiators to conduct the water. A thermostat is used to set the desired temperature. Programmable thermostats respond more efficiently to varying heating and cooling requirements from day to day. Equipment for monitoring and regulating humidity and carbon dioxide levels can also be integrated into the system.

Lots of energy is used to heat and cool our buildings. High efficiency HVAC systems minimize the energy needed to ensure buildings are comfortable. The Energy Star program evaluates HVAC equipment and can help determine the energy savings that may be realized by selecting a particular product. Regular maintenance, such as changing air filters and inspecting equipment, is always needed to maximize efficiency. Ductwork should be checked periodically as well to seal leaks in the system and remove kinks from flexible duct material. If an HVAC system is more than ten years old, it may be helpful to have its efficiency evaluated by a professional. Air speed, air quality, temperature, and humidity can be monitored to optimize thermal comfort and minimize energy use.

A passive system maximizes natural wind resources and does not require the same level of maintenance or electrical power as an active system, but it may not be as efficient in climates with extreme fluctuations in temperature and humidity. Combinations of active and passive ventilation systems are in use today. When a passive system is integrated into a design, a smaller mechanical plant is required. Consulting with professionals will be important to determine what system design works best in your area, given its particular environmental conditions.

Keystone Community Church, St. Gabriel Church, Holy Wisdom Monastery, Temple Emanuel, Pulaski Heights United Methodist Church, and Eldridge Street Synagogue have all installed high efficiency HVAC systems in their buildings. Each community has a well-insulated building and uses operable windows to facilitate natural ventilation. Computer controls make adjustments based on the input from carbon dioxide sensors in the buildings. Keystone's system also includes radiant floor perimeter heating. Radiant heating systems distribute heat in a room by locating either electrical elements or a network of fluid-filled tubing in the flooring. Radiant floor perimeter heating is a system of tubing embedded in the baseboard to provide supplemental heat. Radiant heating systems do not need ductwork, fans, or blowers and have been found to distribute heat uniformly. A radiant system could work well with materials that absorb, store, and radiate thermal energy.

Maximizing Integration at Beth David

Congregation Beth David does not use a central HVAC system but does have a standby heating unit. Extensive computer modeling was done to identify an optimal thermal comfort system that integrates passive and active approaches. The building interior now employs passive features that include a well-insulated building; solar heating through the use of materials that absorb and radiate heat, including concrete shear walls in the sanctuary, concrete masonry walls, straw bale walls with extra plaster, water tanks, and Trombe walls; and operable windows. Each room is equipped with its own thermostat and carbon dioxide sensor, to assist with delivering heating or cooling only as needed. A computer program monitors temperature settings and carbon dioxide levels and controls (opens or closes) nineteen interior transom windows, seven skylights, and 106 exterior windows. Supplemental heat is supplied by wall heaters as needed. To date, the congregation is realizing energy cost savings of 38 percent below the California Title 24 standard, one of the most stringent building codes in the United States. This translates into saving 108,000 kilowatt-hours of electricity annually.

Optimizing Systems at JRC

Jewish Reconstructionist Congregation (JRC) uses passive and active systems. Its building has operable windows around the perimeter that allow for passive cooling and introduce fresh air. Concrete in the floors helps to absorb and radiate solar heat. They have installed a high efficiency HVAC system composed of thirty zones through which to regulate heating and cooling in a more precise, area-specific way. Boilers used in the system are 95 percent efficient. Each room has a separate thermostat and variable air velocity box to deliver warm or cool air. This design allows air to be delivered only to particular rooms as needed. The primary sanctuary uses a displacement ventilation system that circulates the air in such a way that only the bottom seven feet of the room is either warmed or cooled, allowing for a high ceiling without the energy costs of heating or cooling the entire room. Carbon dioxide sensors in each room are integrated into the system to ensure that the correct level of fresh air will be delivered to specific areas as needed. The building is expected to use 42 to 45 percent less energy than a conventional building. With the recent higher costs of fuel, the community has recovered the extra $250,000 in costs associated with installing the high efficiency system in about one-half the time originally expected.

PRODUCT SELECTION

Two important issues affect product selection for interior environments: (1) the source of the products and (2) the level of volatile organic compounds the products release over time. The discussion of sustainable building materials in chapter 6 relates to choosing materials for the interior as well. Materials that have been recovered for reuse, that include recycled content, and that are generated from rapidly renewable sources will contribute to maintaining a more healthy and sustainable environment. Certification programs can help guide product selection and verify the claims of manufacturers.

Factors affecting the sustainability potential for an interior product can be seen in office furniture manufactured by Herman Miller. The company, with headquarters and manufacturing plants in western Michigan, has been committed to care of the environment for decades. Their current sustainability goals, to be met by the year 2020, include the following:

- Zero carbon footprint
- Zero landfill
- Zero hazardous waste generation
- Zero air emissions
- Zero process water use
- 100 percent green electrical energy use
- Company buildings constructed to a minimum LEED Silver certification
- 100 percent of sales from DfE-approved products (Design for the Environment, another certification program)

This level of commitment to environmental stewardship is directly reflected in their products. The company website (www.herman-miller.com) provides environmental information about its products. The recyclability of a product, its recycled and reclaimed content, and specific certifications are noted in its product literature. Environmental product summaries discuss design protocol, certifications achieved, material content, product performance, and LEED credit potential related to the product. Even detailed documents for determining specific LEED credit are provided for many products. (See downloadable documents provided under "Aeron chairs," for an example.) Herman Miller is not the only manufacturing company investing time, energy, and resources into becoming more environmentally responsible. But congregations can encourage their good work, and that of others, by taking time and effort to support vendors who share their concern for creation.

A second important issue related to interior building environments concerns volatile organic compounds (VOCs). VOCs, discussed in chapter 3, decrease air quality in our homes, schools, stores, workplaces, and places of worship. VOCs are chemicals released as gases over time by adhesives used in floor and wall coverings or in manufacturing products, sealants used to fill in gaps and produce a barrier, floor and wall coverings, paints and coatings, stains, wood and agrifiber products (such as doors, countertops, cabinets, and molding), furniture, office equipment, and cleaning supplies. The smell associated with new car interiors and new carpets is attributed to VOCs. Not all VOCs are toxic, but many do negatively affect building occupants. Concentrations of some of the chemicals can build up over time, especially in those environments with minimal ventilation. Health effects associated with VOCs include eye, nose, and throat irritation; headaches; loss of coordination; nausea; and damage to the liver, kidney, and central nervous system.[2] Reactions to VOCs vary widely in the general population, but some of the chemicals that are emitted are known carcinogens. A creation care strategy would seek to eliminate VOCs to the degree possible in interior environments through wise product selection and healthy ventilation.

The quality of the interior environment for religious facilities is affected by a wide variety of products that we might not think about very often. Products include items for worship spaces, classrooms, offices, meeting rooms, libraries, kitchens, dining rooms, and recreation areas. Because our interior environments are more frequently renewed, they can more readily be adapted to meet creation care priorities, even if this vision was not part of the original design.

Low-emitting VOC products of many kinds are available in the marketplace today. Zero-emitting VOC products are emerging as well. Chapter 3 mentioned different programs for verifying environmental claims about interior building materials (for example, the many Scientific Certification Systems programs, Green Seal, and MBDC Cradle to Cradle). VOC status of paints, stains, adhesives, sealants, textiles, wood composites, flooring materials (wood, carpet, cushions, linoleum, and others), classroom and office furniture systems, and seating can all be evaluated. Vendors who submit their products for certification and achieve recognition will identify this mark of environmental stewardship on their products.

Our ten congregations exhibit many wise product choices. Temple Emanuel used bamboo, a rapidly renewal resource, for its flooring in its alternate worship space. The flooring in its classrooms had a recycled materials content level of 80 percent. Countertops in its library are made of wheatboard, a composite material made from agrifiber that contains no formaldehyde. All carpets, stains, and adhesives in the building were rated as low-VOC emitting. St. Gabriel Church has retained marble liturgical furnishings, wooden pews for congregational seating, and stained and etched glass from its original building, a form of product reuse. Throughout their building, they used GreenGuard-certified (another certification system for sustainable products) office and meeting room furnishings, low-VOC carpets with fibers from beets and cornstalks, millwork with wheat strawboard (formaldehyde free), and low-VOC and some zero-VOC stains, adhesives, and sealants. Congregation Beth David retained liturgical furnishings from its previous building. The carpets, stains, adhesives, and sealants they used were low VOC. Holy Wisdom Monastery used bamboo as flooring in its primary worship space and incorporated low-VOC carpets, stains, adhesives, and sealants in their project. Pulaski Heights Church used low-VOC carpets, paints, adhesives, and sealants.

Reclaimed and Recycled Materials as JRC

Jewish Reconstructionist Congregation (JRC) retained some liturgical furnishings from its previous building. The new ark described above included reclaimed and recycled materials. They used a composite material called Dakota Burl for cabinets and shelving in their offices and Early Childhood Center. Agricultural fiber and sunflower hulls are combined to produce a visually textured appearance resembling burled wood. The material emits no VOCs. While JRC did use polished concrete for the majority of its floor surfaces, carpeting was used for offices on the first and second floors. The carpet was made with non-VOC, nonformaldehyde fibers that include both recycled content and rapidly renewable corn content. The stains, adhesives, and sealants used throughout the building are also low VOC.

Restoring the Interior at Eldridge Street

The Eldridge Street synagogue project engaged the services of EverGreene Architectural Arts (www.evergreene.com; offices in New York City, and Oak Park, Illinois) to clean and conserve its painted interior surfaces. Environmental sustainability has been a focus of the firm for more than thirty years. Among other efforts, it has developed a line of environmentally sustainable decorative finishes, the G Series. This series features low-VOC paints and sealants, lime-based plasters, 100 percent recycled postconsumer glass coatings, and salvaged precious metals. The materials developed are earth friendly and durable, encouraging good stewardship of both the environment and finances. All carpets, stains, adhesives, and sealants used in the project were also low VOC.

GREEN WALLS, LIVING WALLS, OR VERTICAL GARDENS

A green or living wall, sometimes called a vertical garden or bio-wall, is a freestanding or integrated wall in a building that is partially or completely planted in vegetation. Green walls may be located on the façade or inside a building. An underlying structure, often of stainless steel, holds containers and the growing medium (engineering soil or inorganic material, available in various forms) for the vegetation. An irrigation system provides water for the plants. Aeroponic plants (those that can grow without soil) can also be used on these walls. Aeroponic plants are suspended in the frame structure. Their roots are exposed to the air and require a misting of nutrient-rich water for growth. Adequate light sources are needed for green walls. Light can be directed to interior walls in multiple ways. A skylight can provide natural illumination. Often adjacent windows will provide natural light as well. Supplemental artificial illumination could be provided, although the spectrum of light necessary for plant growth would need to be accommodated.

Multiple advantages are realized in incorporating green walls. The plants add color and life to our artificial structures. When we encounter them, we are reminded of the plant world all around us, its fragility and resilience. As with green roofs, green walls will absorb solar radiation and help to reduce the overall temperature of the building. The plantings take in the carbon dioxide we exhale and release oxygen. When plants are used inside, the presence of this natural filtering and air renewal feature can be readily discerned. Greywater could be routed for use in green walls too, and the plantings will even process the recycled water to a limited degree. Green walls do require special care and maintenance. Plantings need to be suitable for a vertical scheme, the geographic locale (plants should be indigenous and hardy), and immediate context (outside or inside). Containers, soil, and plumbing require ongoing maintenance. Green walls can remind us of the intimate relationship we have with the world, and tending them might inspire—and train—us to care more readily for plantings of many kinds.

St. Gabriel Church installed a green wall in its narthex. The wall is located on the north end of the space and is about two stories high. A skylight is located above the wall, and windows flank one side to provide ample natural light from the south. The wall is incorporated into a large stairwell from the floor below, creating an attractive entrance from the underground parking area. A metal frame holds the soil material and a host of tropical and semitropical plants. Water runs over the soil to keep the plants appropriately moist. The plants release oxygen that refreshes the air in both the narthex and the worship space. The living wall is a beautiful expression of the created order and a reminder to preserve the fragile dimensions of our natural world.

Detail of green wall at St. Gabriel Church of the Sorrowful Virgin.
(Author photo.)

OCCUPANT COMFORT

Occupants' perception of an interior environment and their ability to regulate lighting, ventilation, and temperature are aspects of occupant comfort that creation care design needs to address. Exposure to natural daylight and outdoor views while inside a building affects a person's perception of the space. Studies indicate that people feel better and productivity improves when they have access to natural light,[3] and being able to see the outside world affects occupants positively. These factors are actually rewarded when groups pursue LEED certification. For example, LEED 2009 will grant credit in the interior environmental quality category when at least 75 percent of regularly occupied spaces have windows and when 90 percent of regularly occupied spaces have views. As people of faith, we should not be surprised to find that we feel better when we experience sunlight and view the beauty of the natural world.

Enabling people to adjust lighting levels and thermal comfort systems is also important. Using excessive lighting can frustrate occupants, unnecessarily reduce the life of lamps, and waste energy. Designing artificial light systems that can automatically adjust to the natural light levels and be adjusted by users can increase occupant comfort. Personal task lighting to illuminate a work area and desk lamps can be useful. Thermal comfort also involves ventilation and temperature preferences. While not every individual in a room may be perfectly accommodated, designs can grant control to occupants by using zone or room thermostats. Simply providing windows that are operable—that can be opened and closed as needed—will give occupants access to fresh air and allow them to adjust room temperature. Operable vents can also be integrated into rooms to allow for individualized adjustment. Periodically verifying the perceived comfort levels of congregational spaces would be a wise practice. Providing communication lines for feedback about how lighting, temperature, and air quality are perceived is essential for optimal occupant comfort. Glitches in a system or nonfunctioning mechanisms can be identified and addressed more quickly in this way. And the occupants will appreciate the attention focused on maintaining an optimal working and living environment.

LIGHTING SYSTEMS

Daylight is the ideal form of interior lighting in our buildings. The importance of harvesting natural daylight and ways in which this can be done using windows, clerestory, skylights, and light convey-ors were noted in chapter 6. While natural daylight can provide a large percentage of interior lighting on sunny days, artificial inte-rior lighting is needed as a supplement for overcast days, nights, and in some interior spaces.

Artificial lighting has become much more efficient in the last couple of decades, yielding a helpful array of bulbs, ballasts, sen-sors, and controls. Average consumers are probably most familiar with the array of compact fluorescent lamp or light (CFL) and light emitting diode (LED) options. CFL bulbs are beginning to find a more substantial place in the consumer market today. They sup-port creation care in that they use less energy and create less heat than conventional incandescent bulbs. According to the Energy Star program, CFLs that earn their rating use about 75 percent less energy than standard incandescent bulbs (saving up to $40 in electricity costs over the lifetime of the bulb), last up to ten times longer, and produce 75 percent less heat (safer to operate and help to cut energy costs associated with building cooling).[4] CFLs vary in their spectrum of light and the time it takes them to achieve maximal brightness. To make the best selection for a particular ap-plication, consult a guide (available through the Energy Star web-site and other sources) and test a variety of bulbs in that location.

A caution about CFLs is that a very small amount of mercury (about four milligrams on average) is found in each bulb. Mercury is a highly toxic substance. If the bulb is broken the mercury will be released into the environment and may pose a health risk. The quantity of mercury in the bulbs is actually quite low (old ther-mometers contained about 500 milligrams of mercury) and newer low-mercury bulbs contain as little as one milligram. Nevertheless, CFLs need to be recycled through appropriate channels rather than thrown in the trash. If a CFL bulb does break, special care must be taken in cleaning up the debris (especially allowing for ad-equate room ventilation and collecting all broken glass and visible powder). Choosing low-mercury CFLs, locating them in fixtures where they are least likely to break, and developing an appropriate procedure for their disposal will minimize the risk of using CFLs and maximize energy savings.[5]

LED lighting is another source for illumination. LEDs are solid light bulbs (also called solid-state lighting), so they do not have the same potential for breakage that conventional or CFL bulbs do. They have been used as indicator lights in many devices since the 1960s. Over the years LED manufacturers have sought to achieve a full-spectrum color, seeking a white light output that could rival the incandescent bulb. Until the past year or two, LEDs have been suitable only for low-light applications (no higher than the equivalent of a forty-watt bulb). New bulbs are brighter, and manufacturers are clustering and packaging LEDs to be used in conventional light sockets. LED technology is promising for several reasons. LEDs are more energy efficient and have a longer lifespan than CFLs. LEDs also appear to be more flexible than CFLs. LEDs can be dimmed more readily than CFLs, and their life expectancy in recessed lighting is not decreased as it is with some CFLs. LEDs do not contain mercury and can be disposed of more easily than CFLs.[6] It may turn out that CFLs are an energy-efficient transition to superior LED options, but until the range of illumination applications can be met through LED alternatives, CFLs are a helpful option.

In the congregational setting, LED options should be considered for low-light applications, such as accent lighting, personal task lighting or desk lamps, and exit signs. LED applications will yield both lower energy costs and less maintenance. The emerging brighter light products are expected to have significant price tags, at least in the early years, but incentives may be developed to make them competitive with incandescent and CFL rivals. An additional advantage to LEDs is that their low energy requirements can more easily be met through the use of solar energy sources.

Conventional linear fluorescent lighting is used in many congregational settings. Where this lighting is used, converting the existing fixtures to high efficiency lamps and ballasts would increase energy efficiency. Smaller diameter, more energy-efficient lamps are available. (T-5 and T-8 will replace T-12. *T* is for "tube," and numerical designations are related to the diameter of the tube—5/8 inch for T-5, 8/8 or one inch for T-8, and 12/8 or 1½ inches for T-12.) T-5 lamps yield superior illumination and are more efficient than T-8 lamps but are more expensive as well. A cost analysis will determine whether T-8 or T-5 lamps would be better for a particular setting. These energy-efficient lamps improve energy savings by about 40 to 50 percent over the T-12 lamp, yield more illumination with better color rendition, and do not flicker. Because the wattage of different lamps varies, it is important to change the ballast in each fixture if the lamp type (for example, from T-12 to T-5) is changed. As with CFLs, linear fluorescent lamps contain small amounts of mercury and must be recycled appropriately.

Many of us are becoming more aware of the fact that lighting for some building spaces is unnecessary or excessive. In congregational settings this can easily occur because of varying schedules for use of the facility in any given week. Automatic controls for lighting can significantly lower energy costs and extend product life. Occupancy sensors detect motion in a space via infrared or ultrasonic sensors. They can be configured to control one or more fixtures and can be mounted on the wall or on a ceiling surface. Timers can be used to regulate both interior and exterior lights. And photosensing devices can adjust the level of artificial illumination based on the amount of natural light in a space. The costs associated with the various automatic control systems can be recovered in a timely fashion through the energy savings that will be achieved.

The lighting needs for a particular congregational setting, given ever-changing technology and products, will be best determined in conversation with others in the community. An energy audit can help establish the amount of energy used for lighting (and HVAC costs) and provide data to evaluate costs and cost-recovery timelines. The US Department of Energy provides guidance for conducting both do-it-yourself and professional assessments.[7] Local utility companies can be of help as well. Incentives for investing in new energy-efficient solutions may emerge and could help underwrite initial costs for products.

St. Gabriel Church uses high efficiency lighting throughout its building, including room occupancy and daylight sensors to control lighting. Congregation Beth David uses motion detectors in all main rooms to control lighting. High efficiency lighting is used throughout the building and the *ner tamid* is solar powered. Jewish Reconstructionist Congregation uses T-5 lamps with dual

controls (to allow fixtures to emit only half the light when necessary) and light sensors throughout its building. The *ner tamid* in
the day chapel and the lamp in the sanctuary are both solar powered. Holy Wisdom Monastery uses high efficiency lighting and
sensors to trigger artificial illumination.

GREEN CLEANING PROGRAMS

Over time our buildings are subject to the forces of nature and
wear from human occupants. The effects of rain, snow, ice, dirt,
and dust, in conjunction with a host of human activities, mean
we need to clean our spaces, inside and outside, for the sake of
both appearance and health. Insects, rodents, and disease-causing
bacteria and viruses of many kinds can contaminate our buildings. Green cleaning is probably not new to most congregations.
Recycling, for example, is a form of green cleaning that many congregations already practice. Recycling reduces the amount of material going to landfills, saves on natural resource consumption,
reduces emissions of greenhouse gases, and reduces the energy
needed to produce new products. This activity leads to new jobs
and manufacturing opportunities.

Green cleaning also encompasses the selection of cleaning
products, choice of equipment, training of personnel who clean,
and cooperation of the building occupants. Cleaning products
may include paper items, such as paper towels and bathroom tis-
sue. The volume of paper products needed should be considered.
For example, might hand dryers in restrooms be preferable to paper towels? And their origin should be determined. For example,
are they from recycled or renewable sources? Trash can liners are
another item to consider. Biodegradable or compostable bags are a
new option in the marketplace.

Billions of pounds of chemicals are used each year in cleaning products for bodies, food-related items, and spaces in our
homes, schools, and working areas. Many of the chemicals in

these products can cause respiratory and dermatological problems in people. Often we do not consider the chemical content of our cleaning products nor do we consider the effects that using those chemicals have on us or their impact on the natural world. A green cleaning strategy in a congregational setting requires an audit of cleaning products and selecting products that are independently certified as sustainable for people and the environment. The certification process for verifying environmental claims noted in chapter 3 also applies to cleaning products. Green Seal (www.greenseal. org), EcoLogo (www.ecologo.org), and the EPA's DfE (Design for the Environment at www.epa.gov/dfe) are examples of programs that provide this service, and information about certified products and the programs can be found on their websites. Cleaning products that have been certified by these parties bear the logo of the program that has made the evaluation. Because more consumers are choosing and using ecofriendly cleaning products, the cost of these products has gone down, making them both competitively priced and readily available.

To promote green cleaning, congregations will need to evaluate, and possibly replace, cleaning equipment. For example, conventional vacuum cleaners can contribute to poor interior air quality, excessive noise levels, and excessive energy consumption. While larger particulates may be removed, smaller airborne dust may simply be circulated throughout the building. Vacuum cleaners in a green cleaning program should be fitted with a HEPA (high efficiency particulate air) filter to trap these small particles. A range of HEPA filters exists on the market today. It is important to select a vacuum cleaner that utilizes a true or absolute HEPA filter to achieve the maximum benefit. Noise output level and energy efficiency are also important. Carpet cleaning equipment requires evaluation as well. Manufacturers are increasingly eager to demonstrate their concern for environmental issues. Certification programs can help determine the type and level of actual benefit.

Green cleaning products need to be used properly. Sometimes people use excessive amounts of a cleaning product, including those that are green, which counters the intent to reduce the volume of chemicals introduced into our environment. Investing in dispensers to measure the product can help ensure appropriate use. Installing touchless fixtures (fitted with motion-detecting sensors) for lighting, water, restroom soap, and hand drying can also reduce the number of surfaces that potentially harbor bacteria and require constant cleaning.

Training those who will implement the green cleaning program will be essential. They will need to understand the reasons for the green protocols and agree to implement them, the particular products and their appropriate use, safe use of equipment, and water and energy conservation measures. A green cleaning program is as beneficial to those who clean as it is to those who occupy the building, minimizing exposure to harmful elements and contributing to a healthier world. Those who occupy the building will need to be aware of the necessity of the green cleaning program as well. Unfamiliar or new ways of living can be difficult to support. The green strategy can be achieved only if the entire community commits to its success.

Recycling is an example of a green cleaning practice that was once unfamiliar but has been slowly becoming an established practice in communities across the country. Many religious communities are investing time and effort in recycling, and it is an important approach to processing community waste. New habits may need to be established in order for recycling to flourish in a faith community. For example, recycling requires members of the community to actively sort and dispose of waste materials in particular ways. Attention to the type of material—sometimes including different types of plastic, paper, metal, and glass—is needed, and the waste must be deposited in the appropriate location. Congregations seeking to promote recycling need to actively discuss its benefits, provide visible and frequent reminders to recycle, and establish multiple locations for deposits. A system for collecting and transferring the gathered materials to the appropriate processing center is also needed if the effort is ultimately to be helpful.

Initiating a green cleaning program in a congregation, regardless of its scope, requires that leaders spearheading the effort focus on benefits and incentives for cooperation. Those who oversee the program will need to attend to product purchasing and will need training. Green housekeeping plans are being implemented by

Keystone Community Church, St. Gabriel Church, Congregation Beth David, Jewish Reconstructionist Congregation, Holy Wisdom Monastery, Temple Emanuel, and Pulaski Heights Church. Each community has an active recycling program as well.

Keystone Community Church café and gathering area. The worship space entrance is on the left and the primary exterior entrance is to the right. A central skylight and large areas of clear glass provide much natural light to the interior. The floor pictured here is polished and stained concrete, a surface that is durable and requires minimal maintenance. A comprehensive green cleaning program is used in the church, including a congregation-wide recycling program. (Author photo.)

FINAL THOUGHTS ON THE INTERIOR ENVIRONMENT

Occupants of buildings are directly affected by unhealthy air, materials, and cleaning products in our built environments. Pursuing creation care in interior spaces will provide some of the most obvious benefits for our congregations. All types of building projects can exercise creation care in their interior spaces. New construction projects will probably achieve the most seamless and cost-effective green interiors, simply because items such as HVAC systems, wall and floor coverings, and artificial lighting are easiest to plan for and install from the beginning of a project. Including systems that will accommodate more individualized or zone preferences will increase occupant comfort and energy efficiency. If a green housekeeping program has been implemented from the outset as well, then there is minimal contamination from less healthy chemicals and cleaning equipment.

Retrofitting a building is a natural process, given the natural deterioration of paint, wall coverings, floor coverings, appliances, storage units, and furniture of all kinds. Technologies change over time as well, which creates opportunities for incorporating new materials and infrastructure in our buildings. Renovating an existing space or restoring and preserving a historical building provide multiple avenues for implementing creation care. High efficiency HVAC and lighting can usually be installed in such projects. There may be limits on the number of options that will be feasible for a given building, but energy-efficient systems that allow for more precise control of air quality and light levels should be possible. And implementing a green housekeeping program can be done in renovation, restoration, and preservation projects. It may take more effort to maintain a green approach to cleaning, especially in an existing space that has been cleaned in particular ways for many years. But with ongoing leadership intentionally emphasizing the importance of green housekeeping and commitment from the entire community, ingrained patterns can gradually change.

Removing hazardous materials, such as those that contain asbestos, arsenic, lead, or mercury, is a benefit of creation care oriented renovation and restoration activities too. Identification and removal of hazardous waste is best done with the assistance of professionals. They can provide guidance in removing and disposing of the contaminated materials properly in your community. Significant strides toward creation care goals can be achieved in and through sustainable interior renovation, restoration, and preservation work.

CHAPTER 8

Creation Care in Motion

The world in which we live is a place of beauty. It contains the resources necessary to sustain life and has the capacity to absorb the waste that living forms produce. The earth's design is truly elegant and often mysterious. Humanity is free to live in ways that disrupt or enhance creation's original design, a design that encourages the flourishing of all life. Making a commitment to greening the life of a faith community is necessary if we are to model our belief that the earth is the Lord's and fulfill our primary charge to serve and protect the creation. Fulfilling the commitment is complex and can be energizing. Pursuing a creation care vision for spaces for worship and ministry is an opportunity for faith communities to assess and intentionally alter our patterns of living in the world. An intentional plan will need to be developed and implemented over an extended period of time in order to fulfill most congregational goals. In this final chapter I will share some concrete suggestions for establishing a plan and caring for creation through our land and buildings.

ACKNOWLEDGING THE NEED

Recognizing the pressure that record population growth yields in the form of increased natural resource consumption and waste production is an important first step in preparing to pursue green building. As congregations active in a living world, we are adding to the pressures that increased human needs exert on existing resources and inevitably producing waste that will need to be reabsorbed into our habitat. Congregations need to begin by acknowledging our contributions to unsustainable patterns of living.

Scripture teaches us many things about the nature of God's world and our place in it. The very gift of this beautiful created world, with its colors, textures, and diversity, is a truth to celebrate. The bounty of resources that it contains and its capacity to support us from generation to generation is a wonder that we need to appreciate. Humanity has been located within a complex web of life. We occupy a unique niche and have been charged with responsibilities to protect and serve the creation as agents of the Creator of all things. The intimate connection that exists between us and God's world means that the ways we choose to respond to God's instructions influence the quality of life of human and nonhuman creatures alike. The gift of creation, our place in that order, and our responsibility to care for all living things are faith affirmations that need to be explored and celebrated in our communities on a regular basis. Humility, thankfulness, and joy are all appropriate postures for embodying these biblical understandings in our congregations.

ESTABLISHING A COMMITMENT

Once we are able to recognize and acknowledge the state of our environment and the opportunities bestowed upon us to act in life-giving ways, we are ready to develop a commitment to green building. Leadership will be needed in our communities to develop

congregation-wide strategies to green our communities and monitor the fulfillment of our goals. Endorsement and ongoing support of green building initiatives will be needed from our leaders
in order to give high priority to the efforts and to build a broad
consensus of support. Establishing a group of members who will
provide direct leadership for congregational creation care is essential. The small group, sometimes called a "green team," should not
be charged with fulfilling all responsibilities of green building in a
congregation (for each member must make a conscious decision
to act in life-renewing ways), but mobilizes others to pursue the
goals that are established. A commitment to green building is not
a temporary measure that can be quickly achieved. Instead, it is a
long-term commitment to a process of renewing goals and plans
in light of measureable growth and ever-unfolding understandings
about the world in which we live.

NETWORKING FOR IDEAS AND SUPPORT

The congregations featured in this book demonstrate that green
building has been a priority for decades in some faith communities
and is relatively new to others. As people of faith who value community, we must acknowledge that we are not alone in our desire
to pursue green initiatives. Inquiries through local faith community networks, web-based networks, or state and local environmental organizations will help us identify others who are pursuing
creation care. Reach out to these communities to establish genuine
connections and to learn from one another about what may be
done within your local or regional context.

Visit the property and buildings of other congregations. It is
especially helpful to actually see the ways in which green building is taking tangible form and to learn about the challenges of
maintaining healthy patterns over time. Different levels of support
for fulfilling creation care—for example, financial incentives, recycling options, energy audits, alternative transit systems, historic
preservation infrastructure—are available in our cities, towns, and
rural areas, and resources for environmental care vary from state

to state and province to province. Through on-site visits you can learn what resources, including building materials, energy and water strategies, waste options, and green housekeeping supplies, are readily available. New ecofriendly resources might emerge in a given geographic area if congregational efforts generate momentum and a demand for those resources.

A community can begin networking by seeking like-minded congregations within a particular tradition, but note that some traditions are farther along than others in fulfilling green building. Be willing to move beyond your particular tradition in seeking models and advice. Related benefits include greater knowledge about the beliefs and practices of other traditions. New friendships between individuals may be forged. As common understandings and goals are identified, anxiety about other traditions may be reduced and mutual respect may result.

Developing a Plan

Green building will be implemented most effectively when the time is taken to develop a comprehensive plan for achieving it. Remember the range of green building that can be pursued, from a minimum of increasing building efficiency to an ideal of assisting the regeneration of the creation. Establish a vision that matches the theological affirmations of the community. Analysis of congregational patterns of consumption and waste (for example, energy and water usage trends, kitchen procedures, transportation modes, supply acquisition, maintenance procedures, waste production and disposal, and so forth) will be important for measuring the present environmental impact of a congregation. The analysis will assist the congregation in identifying concerns for initial improvement and provide benchmarks against which to compare future measurements.

Networking with others will yield information about important ways in which green building can be pursued within your local context. The insights from networking connections can be combined with advice from land development and building professionals. Working with architects, engineers, contractors, and other professionals knowledgeable in green building will help your congregation expand its knowledge of existing strategies, materials, and benefits. Using building rating systems, such as LEED, may assist a congregation in achieving a comprehensive plan and provide external accountability.

Establishing current congregational patterns and consulting with others will suggest concrete changes that could be made to maximize creation care. A range of potential changes will probably be determined, with different changes incurring varying levels of financial investment and return. Considering the initial costs for making changes is important, but it is essential to consider life-cycle cost implications, too. Building professionals can assist you in determining these figures. Only when the full financial impact of building choices is understood should a specific plan be outlined.

Changing lifestyle patterns in a congregation is rarely easy. Consider the time that may be needed to allow members of a congregation to grow into the suggested changes. Exposure to new patterns and grasping the necessity for change will be essential if long-term benefits are to be sustained. Preparing a congregation to make lifestyle changes should begin long before any actual changes are suggested. Preparing a congregation includes understanding and embracing the biblical and theological mandate for pursuing creation care, recognizing the need to share the resources and capacity of the earth with our neighbors near and far, and acknowledging our current unsustainable patterns of living. Assisting members of a congregation in coming to the conclusion that they do indeed need to change some of their life patterns will cultivate a receptive foundation for inviting and embracing new alternatives.

IMPLEMENTING THE PLAN

Implementation of needed change to fulfill the goals of a green building plan will require mobilizing the entire congregation. If creation care remains the vision and passion of only a small number of members, it will be difficult to achieve any measurable level of constructive impact. Evaluate the range of congregants who may have particular skills or experience related to building and land issues. Intentionally invite those members to share in the congregational greening process. For example, seek out architects and engineers to assist with design issues and life-cycle costing, financial professionals to help with cost-benefit analysis and other financial priorities, and landscape professionals to guide landscape development. Mobilize plumbers for assessing water systems, electricians for energy systems, interior design professionals for renewing interior environments, janitorial professionals for maintenance design, and carpenters, painters, and masons to help with appropriate tasks. Help each group of professionals explore the current range of green building options for their area of expertise. Not only will the congregation benefit from the expertise of its members but these professionals will also have an opportunity to grow in their field in and through the creation care efforts of their congregation.

For all members of the congregation, provide opportunities to implement green initiatives. The range of actions that could be pursued is wide. Examples include considering one's form of transportation to the building location, use of water and energy resources in the building, and purchase of materials and supplies for congregational needs; writing guidelines and policies for communal green initiatives; educating the congregation in creation care; and volunteering to assist with the transition of existing land and facilities to green building standards. Identifying ways in which all members of the community can share in pursuing green building will even potentially encourage them to translate these communal efforts into personal green building activities in their homes and workplaces.

EDUCATION AND WORSHIP

Education and worship exert powerful influences upon a congregation and occupy a central role in fulfilling creation care initiatives in congregations. Coordinate these central activities for the faith community with the process of fulfilling the green building goals of the community. Each step outlined above will require educating the entire congregation and can take different forms. Education occurs in exchanges as casual as a spontaneous conversation between two individuals or as formal as a curriculum-driven presentation before an age-appropriate audience. Conference settings, workshops, public forums, camp experiences, tours, community-action events, and worship celebrations all function in ways that educate the participants. The multiplicity of avenues that congregations have available to them for education makes it possible to share understandings related to creation care on a regular basis. Global issues, biblical insights, and possible solutions can all be communicated in creative and lively ways through education.

Worship itself is an additional avenue for participating in green building. In some faith traditions the very act of living is thought of (at least potentially) as an offering of thanks and praise to the Creator of all things. The choices a person makes in how to live in the world, in relationship to all other living beings, is viewed as a part of worship. If this view is held, the lifestyle choices for green building become a part of one's offering to the Divine. In a more specific sense, public and private liturgical activities carry the potential for sharing in creation care. Themes related to the nature of creation and how people are to live in the world are easily integrated into formal or informal worship events. Through the reading and proclamation of Scripture, prayer, singing, and other ritual expressions creation care can be emphasized and celebrated.

Sharing stories is an engaging human activity that can be used in both education and worship. Encourage members to share stories of appreciating the beauty and bounty of the earth, anxiety about resource allocation and waste production, insights about the pursuit of environmental care, and successful implementation of initiatives. Such stories will inspire some to engage in creation care and encourage others to maintain their ongoing commitment. Capitalize on the range of generations in a congregation too. Older members may be able to share a rich mixture of stories about the community's purchase of land and its building projects. The commitment, sacrifices, and unfolding understandings that older generations have experienced will motivate and inform younger members. And a shared sense of purpose and meaning may emerge that reinforces the hopes and dreams for fulfilling a green building program.

May the people of God rise up and take on the challenge of leading our communities in creation care. And may our green building efforts contribute to the renewing of the face of the earth for the sake of God, all who come after us, and the nonhuman creation.

Appendix A

Websites for
Creation Care Resources

Chapter 1 notes a handful of important Jewish and Christian websites to examine for creation care resources. A number of additional websites can be found here. The listing is not exhaustive but represents the variety of sites available to congregations today. Many of the sites are intended specifically for those affiliated with particular expressions of Judaism and Christianity, but there is value in reviewing materials from religious communities beyond one's own congregation. Ideas and applications from other traditions can be useful for multiple settings within a congregation.

Websites for Jewish Congregations

Baltimore Jewish Environmental Network (www.bjen.org) provides numerous resources organized around four program areas: (1) greening synagogues; (2) education and programming; (3) legislative and public policy advocacy;

and (4) engaging the broader Jewish and general communities. The fifteen-page document "Greening Your Synagagoue" (free as a download) provides details about helping a congregation to achieve creation care in community. Special attention is paid to the particularities of the Baltimore area.

Jewish Reconstructionist Federation (JRF) (www.jrf.org) has a host of resources for understanding and embodying creation care. This site's materials are intended for Jewish communities affiliated with Reconstructionist Judaism. The JRF launched a synagogue greening initiative in 2007 and has renewed it each year since its inception. Many resources are available via this website including information about the highest rated Leadership in Energy and Environmental Design (LEED) certified synagogue in the United States. (Based on these criteria for sustainable design developed by the United States Green Building Council, a platinum level rating was awarded Jewish Reconstructionist Congregation, Evanston, Illinois, in September 2009.)

The Orthodox Union (www.ou.org) has a handful of resources for synagogues seeking to fulfill creation care. This site offers materials intended for Jewish communities affiliated with Orthodox Judaism. Examples of materials available through this website are the radio programs (available as MP3 files) in the Journey to Wellness series entitled "Going Green."

The Union for Reform Judaism (www.urj.org) shares a wide array of resources for congregations seeking to be environmentally responsible. This site features materials intended for Jewish communities affiliated with Reform Judaism. One portion of the website (www.urj.org/green/) is dedicated to information that will help congregations learn about and implement healthy environmental stewardship practices. Articles and materials related to the greening of synagogues are also accessible here.

United Jewish Appeal (UJA)-Federation of New York (www. ujafedny.org) is a network of agencies that support social, educational, cultural, recreational, therapeutic, and medical services in the New York City area. They have produced and distribute via their website a comprehensive resource for congregations, *The Greening Guide* (2007), a process for establishing creation care as a congregational priority. Concrete steps for fulfilling a life of stewardship are outlined with numerous links to resources that will help congregations to achieve responsible living in community.

The United Synagogue of Conservative Judaism (www.uscj. org) has multiple resources for affirming creation care and fulfilling stewardship of the environment. This site provides materials intended for Jewish communities affiliated with Conservative Judaism. A movement-wide statement of intent, "Environmental Protection" (2007), as well as sustainability checklists for the home and workplace can be found here. Occasional references and resources can also be found in issues of *Medinat Hagan* (available online).

WEBSITES FOR CHRISTIAN CONGREGATIONS

American Baptist Churches, USA (www.abc-usa.org) has issued a policy statement, "Creation and the Covenant of Caring" (1989; modified 2007) for its churches and provides additional denominational statements and resolutions concerning care for the environment.

The Christian Church (Disciples of Christ) (www.disciples. org) has challenged its churches with its Alverna Covenant (1981) and General Assembly resolutions concerning ecology (from the 1970s to today). They also have Green Building Services and other resources for implementing ecological stewardship.

Church of the Brethren (www.brethren.org) released the statement "Creation: Called to Care" at its 1991 Annual

Conference and has posted other denominational statements and resources encouraging creation care on its
website.

Church of the Nazarene (www.nazarene.org) has links on its
denominational website to articles addressing various aspects of creation care. A more comprehensive guide to its
theological affirmations and suggestions for responsible
stewardship can be found in its recent publication, *Creation
Care: Environmental Stewardship for the Church of the
Nazarene* (Kansas City, MO: Nazarene Compassionate
Ministries, 2005).

The Episcopal Ecological Network (www.eenonline.org) has
links to denominational and diocesan resolutions back to
1977 as well as a host of educational materials and action
links for the Episcopal Church.

The Evangelical Lutheran Church in American (www.elca.
org) released "Caring for Creation: Vision, Hope, and
Justice" (1993) as a denominational policy statement. The
Environmental Education and Advocacy Program has been
established to inform and resource Lutheran congregations
in fulfilling their commitment to creation care.

The Greek Orthodox Archdiocese of America (www.goarch.
org/en/ourfaith/environment) released "The Orthodox
Churches and the Environment" (1991) and shares many
other articles on the environment and the Orthodox
Christian Church from the 1980s to today via its website.

The Mennonite tradition has developed the Mennonite
Creation Care Network (www.mennocreationcare.org) for
distributing resources to promote education for and engagement of stewardship of the earth. In 1995 the denominational statement "The Creation and Calling of Human
Beings" was adopted, which calls for responsible environmental stewardship. Many resources, stories, and links can
be found via the Mennonite network. Also, the Mennonite
Central Committee (www.mcc.org) has numerous resources to promote creation care via its website.

The Presbyterian Church (USA) (www.pcusa.org) issued the denominational statement "Restoring Creation for Ecology and Justice" at its general assembly in 1990. An Environmental Ministries page has been developed for its website that includes denominational resolutions back to the 1970s and many other resources. An additional array of materials can be found at the affiliated Presbyterians for Earth Care website, an ecojustice network site formerly called Presbyterians for Restoring Creation (www.presby-earthcare.org).

The Reformed Church in America (www.rca.org) has a Caring for Creation web page with multiple documents and links for pursuing environmental stewardship.

The Roman Catholic Church in the United States has promoted creation care formally through the United States Conference of Catholic Bishops (www.usccb.org). *Renewing the Earth: An Invitation to Reflection and Action on Environment in Light of Catholic Social Teaching* was released by the US Conference of Catholic Bishops (1991). The Environmental Justice Program (from 1993) has a link on the website that provides many resources for exploring and achieving earth care.

The Society of Friends has established Quaker Earthcare Witness (www.quakerearthcare.org) as a website for resourcing its communities of faith in stewardship of the earth.

The Southern Baptist Convention (www.sbc.net) has posted on its website an article on their Ethics and Religious Liberty Commission, "Environmental Stewardship: A Theological Model for the Environment" by Andrew A. Lewis (2005), for guiding their congregations in considering environmental issues.

The Unitarian Universalist Association has established a Ministry for Earth website (www.uuministryforearth.org). Comprehensive initiatives such as the Green Sanctuary Program (from 1989) and the *Green Sanctuary Manual*, 5th ed., 2009 (from 1991) may be found here.

The United Church of Christ (www.ucc.org) has issued a Faith and Environment document, "And Indeed It Is Very Good: A Pastoral Letter on Faith and Environment—Living in Community with God's Creation" (2008), and provides multiple other documents, including denominational statements, initiatives, bulletin inserts, and so forth, via its site.

The United Methodist Church (www.umc.org) has affirmed and released an Environmental Stewardship resolution (1984; revised and readopted 2000; readopted 2008) and renewed its commitment to environmental care through the Council of Bishops in "God's Renewed Creation: Call to Hope and Action" (2009). Additional resolutions and Faith in Action articles are available at the denominational website.

Church and Synagogue Design as Creation Care: Building Contrast Table

NEW CONSTRUCTION PROJECTS	LAND DEVELOPMENT	BUILDING SHELL	INTERIOR ENVIRONMENT
Keystone Community Church **655 Spaulding Ave.** **Ada, MI 49301** **616-957-2244** 33,000 sq. ft. Approx. cost: $3,000,000 Location: Ada, MI (35 acres) Date completed: 2004 Consulting firm: Integrated Architecture, Grand Rapids, MI LEED notes: LEED certified, basic level, 2005; first worship space in the U.S.	- Minimal site disturbance - Building on a natural meadow - Oriented toward heavy northern woods - Preservation of wetlands - Parking area close to natural grade - Grass swale & wetlands created to assist with storm-water management - No potable water irrigation (use water from retention ponds) - Alternative transportation (bicycle & electric) - Drought-resistant plantings, wildflower field, & low maintenance lawn - Site lighting focused downward (light pollution reduction)	- Two stories high; built on two levels - Construction waste diverted from landfill - South-facing façade with extensive glazing & deep porch - Maximize natural light - Maximize natural views - Use of recycled building materials - Fabricated brick (from local sources) - Precast concrete (from local sources) - Interior precast panels can be reused for future expansion - Prefinished fiber reinforced siding - Polished, stained concrete floor	- Low-flow water fixtures - Waterless urinals - Low-VOC carpets, stains, adhesives, & composite wood products - Lighting controls in building & parking areas - High efficiency HVAC systems - Radiant floor perimeter heating - Maximize fresh air - Operable interior windows in classrooms - Carbon dioxide sensors - Green housekeeping plan - Use reusable coffee mugs & water glasses - Recycle stations for congregation: cardboard, paper (multiple types), plastic, tin, aluminum, clear glass, household batteries, printer cartridges, & fluorescent bulbs - Development of educational program to feature building sustainability

| St. Gabriel of the Sorrowful Virgin Church
670 Sheppard Ave. East
Toronto, ON M2K 1B7
CANADA
416-221-8866

21,500 sq. ft.
Approx. cost: $10,500,000
Location: North York, Toronto, ON (2 acres)
Date completed: July 2006
Consulting firm: Larkin Architects, Roberto Chiotti (lead architect) with Kevin Weiss
LEED notes:
LEED certified, gold level, 2006; first church in Canada to receive this level of certification | - Underground parking, primarily, for 113 vehicles; some handicapped, carpool, & hybrid-vehicle parking near the church
- Extensive garden area on the south side, with drought-resistant plantings & drip-irrigation system
- Site waste diversion from landfill
- Alternative transportation (bicycle & electric vehicles) | - Oriented along a north-south axis
- South-facing façade with extensive glazing & deep cantilevered roof extension
- Maximizes natural light
- Maximizes natural views
- Use of recycled materials (slag in concrete & steel for reinforcement)
- Maximal insulation
- Use of concrete mass for storing, releasing thermal energy
- Passive solar heating
- Purchase of green energy from local utility
- Rainwater recovery system from roof, incorporated into a water feature before going to support irrigation | - "Living wall" installation in the narthex
- High efficiency HVAC systems
- Carbon dioxide sensors
- Maximize natural ventilation
- High efficiency lighting
- Lighting sensors
- Low flow water fixtures
- Dual-flush toilets
- Waterless urinals
- Low-VOC & some zero-VOC carpets, stains, adhesives, & sealants
- Carpets with fibers from beets & cornstalks
- Wheat strawboard in all millwork (formaldehyde free)
- GreenGuard-certified office & meeting room furnishings
- Use of furnishings from previous church
- Green housekeeping plan |

New Construction Projects	Land Development	Building Shell	Interior Environment
Congregation Beth David 10180 Los Osos Valley Rd San Luis Obispo, CA 93405 805-544-0760 16,190 sq. ft. Approx. building cost: $2,524,000 or $156/sq. ft. Location: San Luis Obispo, CA (92 acres; 13 acres developed) Date completed: December 2006 Consulting firm: San Luis Sustainability Group, Santa Margarita, CA (Ken Haggard, Polly Cooper, and Richard Beller, lead architects) LEED notes: LEED certified, basic level, 2008; first synagogue to be certified	- Site waste diversion from landfill - Minimal land development (13 of 92 acres) - Alternative transportation (bicycles) - Wetland development & open space (62 acres) - Drought-resistant indigenous plantings, including a recovery program for a threatened plant species - 10-foot high landscaped berm - Bioswales used for storm-water management - Nesting boxes for barn owls (natural pest control)	- East-west axis of the building capitalizes on southern exposure - Maximizes natural light - Skylights, light shelves, & solar tubes - Maximizes natural views - Maximal insulation, including recycled newsprint - R-35 straw bale walls on two coldest walls - Passive solar heating (147 windows on southern façade, with 11 water tanks & two Trombe walls) - Solar energy production through photovoltaic panels on roof; provides 50% of electric needs	- No central HVAC unit - Thermostats & CO2 sensors in each room - Individual gas fireplaces for supplemental heat in each room - Maximizes natural ventilation - Computer program for monitoring heating & cooling needs; including opening/closing transom windows (19 of 22), exterior windows (106 of 194), & skylights - High efficiency lighting - Lighting sensors - Low-flow water fixtures - Low-VOC carpets, stains, & adhesives - Green housekeeping plan

Jewish Reconstructionist Congregation 303 Dodge Ave. Evanston, IL 60202 847-328-7678 31,600 sq. ft. Approx. construction cost: $7,300,000 Location: Evanston, IL Date completed: February 2008 Consulting firm: Ross Barney Architects, Chicago (Michael A. Ross, lead architect) LEED notes: LEED certified, platinum level, 2008; first religious building & synagogue to receive platinum)	- Demolished existing building (most of the building used to fill in the old basement) - Site waste diversion from landfill (96% of previous synagogue building was recycled) - Solar-powered parking lot lights - No-irrigation landscaping of indigenous & adaptive drought-resistant plants - Gabion walls on exterior contain reclaimed material & Jerusalem stone - Alternative transportation (bicycling, carpooling, mass transit) - Playground mulch from recycled rubber tires	- Ceremonial entry & door with reclaimed maple from site - Maximize natural light (clerestory windows, light shelves, solar tubes) - White, reflective surface on roof - Maximize natural views - Recycled, reclaimed, & rapidly renewable building materials (47% of all materials were made within 500 miles; 50% of all wood used was reused or FSC certified, including recycled barn wood & reclaimed cypress for the exterior; reclaimed cypress also used in the day chapel & main sanctuary; reclaimed black walnut used in the main sanctuary; recycled steel used for beams) - Maximize insulation (insulation material includes recycled glass) - High efficiency windows: insulated, double glazed, gas filled, low-E coating; operable windows around the perimeter - Polished concrete flooring on three levels (recycled fly ash in the floor concrete) - Purchase green energy	- High efficiency HVAC systems (displacement ventilation system in the sanctuary) - Each room has a thermostat & variable air velocity box to deliver warm & cool air - Carbon dioxide sensors - Maximize natural ventilation - High efficiency lighting - Lighting sensors - Two *ner tamid* (eternal light) powered by solar energy - Low-flow water fixtures - Dual-flush toilets - Low-VOC paints, sealants, & adhesives - Nonformaldehyde, non-VOC fiber carpets & recycled material in the carpets used in offices on the first & second floors - Torah ark made of reclaimed & environmentally friendly materials - Cabinets & shelving made with Dakota Burl composite - Green housekeeping plan - Energy Star appliances - Use reusable glasses, cups, plates, bowls, & utensils - Congregational recycling program

New Construction Projects	Land Development	Building Shell	Interior Environment
Holy Wisdom Monastery 4200 County Road M Middleton, WI 53562 608-836-1631 34,000 sq. ft. Approx. cost: $8,000,000) Location: Middleton, WI (138 acres) Date completed: 2009 Consulting firm: Hoffman, Appleton, WI LEED notes: LEED certified, platinum level, 2010; first Christian congregation to receive platinum & highest number of points yet awarded, 63 out of 69)	- Demolished existing building - Site waste diversion from landfill (99.75 %) - Storm-water runoff reduced to 13% below predevelopment levels - Pervious concrete in some parking areas - Indigenous plantings (prairie restoration), drought resistant - Rain gardens - No irrigation system needed - Highly reflective pavers - Overall, highland prairie restoration of 100 acres & glacial lake restoration	- White membrane roof - Vegetated roof - Maximize natural light (daylight to 85% of interior spaces) - Skylights & solar tubes - Maximize natural views (direct line-of-sight views to 99.5% of interior spaces) - Photovoltaic panels (provide 13% of energy needed; goal to provide 100% energy) - Solar light fixtures in parking area - Ground source energy system, 39 wells (each 300 ft. deep) - Purchase 100% green energy from local utility - Rapidly renewable materials (10% of materials) - Forest Stewardship Council certified wood (59.73% of all wood) - Recycled materials (21% of total material costs) - Local/regional materials (28% of total material costs) - Reused materials (12.5% of total material costs)	- High efficiency HVAC systems - Carbon dioxide sensors - Maximize natural ventilation - Operable windows, including clerestory - High efficiency lighting - Lighting sensors - Low-flow water fixtures - Dual-flush toilets - Waterless urinals - Low-VOC carpets, stains, adhesives, & sealants - Rapidly renewable flooring (bamboo) in worship space - Organizational recycling program - Green housekeeping plan - Developed educational program to feature building sustainability

Renovation and Expansion Projects	Land Development	Building Shell	Interior Environment
Temple Emanuel **10101 Connecticut Ave.** **Kensington, MD 20895** **301-942-2000** Expansion & renovation to existing building Location: Kensington, MD (5 acres) Date completed: 2002 Consulting firm: Schwartz & Peoples Architects, Washington, DC (Robert Schwartz, lead architect)	- Site waste diversion from landfill - Minimal site disturbance - Administrative wing half below grade - Comprehensive landscaping plan with indigenous, drought-resistant plantings - Alternative transportation (bicycles)	- Maximal insulation (including upgrading in existing building) - High efficiency windows: double glazed with low-E coating - Purchase green energy from local utility - Regular energy audits - Regular contributions to the Carbonfund	- High efficiency HVAC systems - Carbon dioxide sensors - Maximize natural ventilation - High efficiency lighting - Low-flow water fixtures - Wheatboard countertops in library - Rapidly renewable flooring in alternate worship space (bamboo) - Flooring of recycled material (80%) in classrooms - Low-VOC carpets, stains, & adhesives - Green strategies for food purchasing & kitchen waste disposal - Recycling program - Green housekeeping plan

RENOVATION AND EXPANSION PROJECTS	LAND DEVELOPMENT	BUILDING SHELL	INTERIOR ENVIRONMENT
Annunciation of the Mother of God Byzantine Catholic Church **14610 South Will Cook Rd** **Homer Glen, IL 60491** **708-645-0241** Location: Homer Glen, IL (10 acres) Date completed: 2003 Consulting firm: Conservation Design Forum, Elmhurst, IL	- Site redevelopment - Permeable paving in entry drive & parking area - Pedestrian & bicycle trails across property connect surrounding residential developments - Prairie restoration & indigenous plantings - Storm-water management, including vegetated swales & plant systems - Wetlands development, including a water garden - Nesting boxes for bluebirds	- Green roof for existing church building - Rainwater recovery system from roof to support irrigation	- High efficiency HVAC - Some high efficiency lighting with CFLs - Low-flow features in some fixtures - Congregational recycling program - Green housekeeping program (pending)
Pulaski Heights United Methodist Church **4823 Woodlawn** **Little Rock, AR 72205** **501-664-3600** Nixon Disciple Center: 38,000 sq. ft., 2-story parking deck, & columbarium for phase one of master plan, 2003–2005 Approx. cost: $10,000,000 Location: Little Rock, AR (approx. 4.7 acres) Date completed: 2005 Consulting firm: Cromwell Architects Engineers, Little Rock LEED notes: LEED certified, basic level, 2006	- Site waste diversion from landfill - Water efficient landscaping - Alternative transportation (bicycles) - Site lighting focused downward	- Maximum insulation - Recycled materials for building - Local materials for building - Certified forest wood & products - High efficiency windows—insulated, double glazed, gas filled, low-E coating - Highly reflective roof treatment	- High efficiency HVAC systems - Thermostats in each room - Maximize natural ventilation - High efficiency lighting - Low-flow water fixtures - Waterless urinal (being tested) - Low-VOC carpets, paints, adhesives, & sealants - Green housekeeping program - Congregational education program

HISTORIC PRESERVATION PROJECTS	LAND DEVELOPMENT	BUILDING SHELL	INTERIOR ENVIRONMENT
Museum at Eldridge Street/Eldridge Street Synagogue 12 Eldridge Street New York, NY 10002 212-219-0888 Restoration of synagogue Approx. cost: $18,500,000 Location: New York City (Manhattan, Lower East Side; approx. 5,250 sq. ft. or 0.12 acres) Date completed: 2007 Consulting firm: Walter Sedovic Architects (Jill H. Gotthelf, lead architect)	Site waste diversion from landfill	- Maximize insulation - Restored operable windows - Maximize natural light (skylights & clerestory windows) - Durable materials used/restored (brick & stone) - Recycled building materials	- High efficiency HVAC systems - Maximize natural ventilation - High efficiency lighting in select areas - Lighting sensors - Low-flow water fixtures - Low-VOC carpets, stains, finishes, adhesives, & sealants
Unity Temple 875 Lake Street Oak Park, IL 60301 707-848-6225 Restoration of church Approx. cost: $20–25 million Location: Oak Park, IL (approx. 17,000 sq. ft. or 0.39 acres) Date completed: ongoing Consulting firm: Harboe Architects, Chicago	Site waste diversion from landfill Alternative transportation (bicycles)	- Maximize natural light - Maximize natural ventilation through operable windows - Low-E glass used for covering original skylights - Ground source energy system, one test well (300 ft. deep) - Preparing for geothermal HVAC system	- High efficiency lighting, including CFLs & fluorescent tubes - Green housekeeping plan - Wash food service items in place of disposal ware - Congregational recycling program - Congregational purchasing program for recycled paper products, plastic items, & fair trade & organic products - Use of worm bin for organic waste

Notes

CHAPTER 1: GOD, HUMANITY, AND THE EARTH: INTERCONNECTED AND INTERDEPENDENT

1. See the bibliography for recent examples of substantial works on faith and environmental care from Jewish and Christian perspectives.
2. Thirty-nine books are found in the Tanakh, all of which are found in the collections of Scripture affirmed by Christian communities.
3. I recognize that the language used in the JPS translation is not gender sensitive. To preserve the integrity of this authorative text, I have retained the original language. An alternative language sensitive edition of the translation is also available: *The Contemporary Torah: A Gender-Sensitive Adaptation of the JPS Translation* (2006).
4. W. Gunther Plaut, ed., *The Torah: A Modern Commentary* (New York: Union of Hebrew Congregations, 1981), 22.
5. For commentary along these lines see: S. R. Hirsch, *Hirsch Humash: The Pentateuch* (London: Isaac Levy Publishers, 1962); Genesis 1:26–28; Jeremy Benstein, *The Way into Judaism and the Environment* (Woodstock, VT: Jewish Lights Publishing, 2006), 42–47; and Ellen Bernstein, *The Splendor of Creation: A Biblical Ecology* (Cleveland: Pilgrim Press, 2005), 103–6.
6. Kristin M. Swenson, "Care and Keeping East of Eden: Gen 4:1–16 in Light of Gen 2–3," *Interpretation* 60, 4 (October 2006): 373–84. For an extended discussion of this idea, see H. Paul Santmire, *Ritualizing Nature: Renewing Christian Liturgy in a Time of Crisis* (Minneapolis: Fortress Press, 2008); 205–15.

7. Benstein, *Way into Judaism*, 52–53.

8. Robert E. Wallace, *The Narrative Effect of Book IV of the Hebrew Psalter* (New York: Peter Lang, 2007); 74.

9. Arthur Waskow has written many articles through the years on the benefits of sabbath living for life today in. An accessible source for inspiring environmental care in relation to faith-inspired rhythms can be found in Arthur Waskow, *Seasons of Our Joy: A Modern Guide to the Jewish Holidays* (Boston: Beacon Press, 1982).

10. David Ehrenfeld and Philip J. Bentley, "Judaism and the Practice of Stewardship," in *Judaism and Environmental Ethics: A Reader*, ed. Martin D. Yaffe (Lanham, MD: Lexington Books, 2001), 133.

11. Ibid., 131.

12. Samson Raphael Hirsch, *Horeb: A Philosophy of Jewish Laws and Observances*, trans. I. Grunfeld (New York: Soncino Press, 1981), 279–80.

13. For an extended discussion of this understanding, please see: Steven Bouma-Prediger, *For the Beauty of the Earth: A Christian Vision for Creation Care*, 2nd ed. (Grand Rapids: Baker Academic, 2010), 68–69.

14. M. Eugene Boring, *Revelation* (Louisville: Westminster/John Knox, 1989), 220.

15. Additional detail concerning COEJL activities and Jewish initiatives for environmental concern can be found in Mark X. Jacobs, "Jewish Environmentalism: Past Accomplishments and Future Challenges," in *Judaism and Ecology: Created World and Revealed Word*, ed. Hava Tirosh-Samuelson (Cambridge, MA: Harvard University Press, 2002), 449–80.

16. *Tu B'Shvat* is a holiday celebrated on the fifteenth of the month of Shvat in the Jewish calendar, which usually falls in the last half of January to early February in the Gregorian calendar. In Leviticus 19:23–25 God's people are instructed in how to tithe of the fruit trees in the land. Tu B'Shvat was originally a day on which to mark the beginning of a new fiscal year for tithing. Although not all faith communities continue to observe this original fiscal function of Tu B'Shvat, the holiday continues to be celebrated by eating new fruit and planting trees. In recent years Tu B'Shvat has even been celebrated as a Jewish Earth Day with emphasis on environmental awareness and ecological restoration activities. Reflections on this celebration may be found in: Ari Elon, Naomi Mara Hyman, and Arthur Waskow, eds., *Trees, Earth and Torah: A Tu B'Shvat Anthology* (Philadelphia: Jewish Publication Society, 1999).

17. For example, they publish and distribute *Greening Congregations Handbook: Stories, Ideas, and Resources for Cultivating Creation Awareness and Care in Your Congregation*, a 225-page document via their website.

Chapter 2: Cultivating Creation Care Consciousness

1. NOVA, "Human Numbers through Time," at the PBS website http://www.pbs.org/wgbh/nova/earth/global-population-growth.html.
2. Natural resources are of two kinds: renewable, such as trees and wildlife, and nonrenewable, such as minerals, oil, and coal. Proper management of renewable resources is needed in order to maintain required supplies of materials for existing population demands. Proper management of nonrenewable resources is needed in order that healthy extraction, safe processing, and maximum efficiency of their use is achieved. Faith communities must consider the need to ensure equitable distribution and minimize environmental impact as they determine how to live individually and corporately in the world.
3. Available through the PowerPoint presentation "Building Impacts: Why Build Green?" at US Green Building Council website http://www.usgbc.org/DisplayPage. aspx?CMSPageID=1720.
4. Ibid.
5. Indicated via data found on the websites of Redefining Progress (www.ecologicalfootprint.org) and the Global Footprint Network (www.footprintnetwork.org).
6. United States Forest Service, "About us," http://www.fs.fed.us/aboutus.
7. National Park Service, "About us," http://www.nps.gov/aboutus.
8. Federal legislation prior to 1970 includes the Refuse Act (1899), Federal Water Pollution Control Act (1948), Air Pollution Control Act (1955), Clean Air Act (1963), Solid Waste Disposal Act (1965), Water Quality Act (1965), and the Air Quality Act (1967). Federal attempts to limit pollution related to waste disposal and water and air quality have been developed in relation to the growth of industry since 1899. Recognition of these policies can inspire our congregations to recognize the significance of environmental damage and see our own creation care efforts as part of a larger national initiative.

9. Environmental Protection Agency, "Greenhouse Gas Emissions," http://www.epa.gov/climatechange/emissions/index.html.

10. Ibid.

11. "GSS Health and Sustainability Guide," available online as a free PDF file at Faith for the Common Good, Greening Sacred Spaces website, http://www.greeningsacredspaces.net/files/GSS%20Health%20and%20Sustainability%20Guide-Greening%20Daily%20Operation%20for%20Faith%20Communities.pdf.

12. *The Green Faith Guide: Working Together to Protect and Restore Our Environment,* available online as a free PDF file at Greater Washington Interfaith Power and Light website, http://gwipl.org/go-green/green-congregation-guides/. Multiple congregational guides are available through this site.

13. *Rejoice in Your Handiwork, Sacred Space and Synagogue Architecture, Part Two: Form and Function, Design Considerations for Congregations,* available online as a free PDF file at the Union for Reform Judaism website, http://www.urjbooksandmusic.com/product.php?productid=10086&cat=0&page=70.

14. "Room by Room Greening Guide," available online for free at the Union for Reform Judaism website, http://urj.org/green/building/checklist/?syspage=document&item_id=21720

15. *Building a Firm Foundation: A Creation-Friendly Building Guide for Churches,* available online as a free PDF file at the National Council of Churches of Christ, Eco-Justice Programs website, http://www.nccecojustice.org/resources/index.php#greenbuildingresources.

16. *Green Shalom Action Guide,* available online as a free PDF file at Temple Emanuel, Kensington, Maryland, website, http://www.templeemanuelmd.org/_kd/Items/actions.cfm?action=Show&item_id=1162&destination=ShowItem.

17. *Environmental Guide for Congregations, Their Buildings, and Grounds,* available online as a free PDF file at Web of Creation website, http://www.webofcreation.org/Environmental%20Guide.pdf.

18. *The Greening Guide,* available online as a free PDF file at UJA Federation of New York website, http://www.ujafedny.org/get/61480/download.

19. *Green Sanctuary Manual,* available online as a free PDF file at Unitarian Universalist Association of Congregations website, http://www.uua.org/leaders/environment/greensanctuary/118741.shtml.

CHAPTER 3: GREEN SYNAGOGUE AND CHURCH BUILDING AS CREATION CARE

1. 7group and Bill Reed, *The Integrative Design Guide to Green Building: Redefining the Practice of Sustainability* (Hoboken, NJ: John Wiley and Sons, 2009), 44–46.
2. Environmental Protection Agency, "Green Building: Why Build Green?" http://www.epa.gov/greenbuilding/pubs/whybuild. htm.
3. Environmental Protection Agency, "Green Building: Basic Information," http://www.epa.gov/greenbuilding/pubs/about. htm.
4. Environmental Protection Agency, "Indoor Air Facts No. 4 (revised) Sick Building Syndrome," http://www.epa.gov/ied-web00/pubs/sbs.html.
5. William McDonough and Michael Braungart, *Cradle to Cradle: Remaking the Way We Make Things* (New York: North Point Press/Farrar, Straus and Giroux, 2002).
6. "Putting Energy into Stewardship Congregations Guide," available at Energy Star program website, http://www.energystar.gov/index.cfm?c=congregations_guidebook.
7. A very helpful introduction to LEED and Green Globes can be found in *Understanding Green Building Guidelines for Students and Young Professionals* by Traci Rose Rider (New York: W. W. Norton and Company, 2009). A comprehensive overview of each program is provided in language that is accessible. Additional national and local programs intended to guide green building (including the National Association of Home Builders Green Building Program) are included in this book as well.
8. United States Green Building Council, "About USGBC," http:// www.usgbc.org.
9. United States Green Building Council, "LEED Projects and Case Study Directory," http://www.usgbc.org/LEED/Project/CertifiedProjectList.aspx. I am including the following currently certified projects in faith communities in case of an opportunity for you to visit one of them: Emerson Unitarian Universalist Church, Houston, Texas; Faith United Methodist Church, Champaign, Illinois; First Unitarian Church, Portland, Oregon; Ankeny First United Methodist Church, Ankeny, Iowa; Christ United Methodist Church, Plano, Texas; First Baptist Church, Greenville, South Carolina; Saddleback Church, Lake Forest, California; St. Thomas More Catholic Church, Coralville, Iowa; St. Elizabeth Ann Seton Catholic

Church, Hiawatha, Iowa; St. Patrick Catholic Church, Iowa City, Iowa; the Unitarian Universalist Church of Fresno, Fresno, California.

10. United States Green Building Council, "Research Publications" web page, http://www.usgbc.org/DisplayPage.aspx?CMSPageID=77.

11. For example, Urban Green Council, "Cost of Green in NYC," 2009; Lisa Fay Matthiessen and Peter Morris, "The Cost of Green Revisited," Davis Langdon Consultants, July 2007; Peter Morris, "What Does Green Really Cost?" Davis Langdon Consultants, Summer 2007; US General Services Administration, "GSA LEED Cost Study," 2004; Lisa Fay Matthiessen and Peter Morris, "Costing Green: A Comprehensive Cost Database and Budgeting Methodology," Davis Langdon Consultants, July 2004; G. Syphers et al., "Managing the Cost of Green Buildings," KEMA, October 2003.

12. Peter Morris, "What Does Green Really Cost?," Davis Langdon Consultants, *PREA Quarterly* (Summer 2007): 58.

13. United States Green Building Council, "Building Impacts" presentation "Why Build Green?" at http://www.usgbc.org/DisplayPage.aspx?CMSPageID=1720. The presentation may be downloaded for free and could be very helpful for sharing reasons to pursue green building in a congregational setting.

14. Robert A. Young, *Historic Preservation Technology* (Hoboken, NJ: John Wiley and Sons, 2008), 3.

15. National Park Service, "Introduction to Standards and Guidelines. Introduction: Choosing an Appropriate Treatment for the Historic Building," http://www.nps.gov/history/hps/tps/standguide/overview/choose_treat.htm.

16. The National Trust for Historic Preservation website as a case study for sustainable preservation, "Trinity Church in the City of Boston" (PDF document): http://www.preservationnation.org.

Chapter 4: Models for Creation Care Building and Renovation

1. St. Gabriel's has been featured in multiple articles including Roberto Chiotti, "The Architecture of Eco-Theology," *Faith and Form* 41, no. 1 (2008): 6–11; Roberto Chiotti, "Colouring Your New Church Green," *Celebrate!* 45, no. 5 (September–October 2006): 4–7; Roberto Chiotti, "LEEDing the Way: The

New St. Gabriel's Church," *Celebrate!* 45, no. 6 (November–December 2006): 3–6; Ontario Cast-In-Place Concrete Development Council, "St. Gabriel's Passionist Church," *Case Study 5*, no. 1 (n.d.).

2. Congregation Beth David is featured in multiple publications including Livia D. Thompson, "Where You LEED, I Will Follow," *NATA Journal* 43, no. 2 (Fall 2008/5769): 6–9, and Union for Reform Judaism, *Rejoice in Your Handiwork: Sacred Space and Synagogue Architecture*, Part Two (New York: Union for Reform Judaism, 2005), 38.

3. See: David A. Bainbridge and Ken Haggard, *Passive Solar Architecture: Heating, Cooling, Ventilation, Daylighting and More Using Natural Flows* (White River Junction, VT: Chelsea Green, 2011), and Ken Haggard, David A. Bainbridge, and Rachel Aljilani, *Passive Solar Architecture Pocket Reference* (Oxford, UK: EarthScan/Taylor and Francis, 2010).

4. Fractal architecture is based on seeking inspiration from ordinary irregularity in patterns in nature. The algorithms that describe irregularity in geometric patterns (fractals) in nature are examined and applied to design. For more information, see: Ken Haggard and Polly Cooper, *Fractal Architecture: Design for Sustainability* (Charleston, SC: BookSurge, 2006).

5. Jewish Reconstructionist Congregation has been featured in multiple journals including Thompson, "Where You LEED, I Will Follow," 6–9.

6. The work of Temple Emanuel has been identified as a catalyst for sustainable living in Sheryl Lechner, "A DC Temple's Quest to Live Lightly on the Earth," *Reform Judaism* (Summer 2005): 41–42, 44–45.

7. The history and significance of Eldridge Street Synagogue has been documented in Annie Polland, *Landmark of the Spirit: The Eldridge Street Synagogue* (New Haven, CT: Yale University Press, 2009).

8. The history and design of Frank Lloyd Wright and Unity Temple can be explored in more detail in Joseph M. Siry, *Unity Temple: Frank Lloyd Wright and Architecture for Liberal Religion* (Cambridge, UK: Cambridge University Press, 1998), and Patrick F. Cannon and James Caulfield, *Frank Lloyd Wright's Unity Temple: A Good Time Place* (Petaluma, CA: Pomegranate Communications, 2009). Additional insight into the life of the congregation can be found in Ron Moline, *In Good Faith: Compiled from the Archives of the Unity Temple Unitarian Universalist Congregation of Oak Park* (Bloomington, IN: Xlibris, 2008).

CHAPTER 5: THE LAND WE OCCUPY

1. Jerry Yudelson, *Greening Existing Buildings* (New York: McGraw Hill, 2010), 151–52.

CHAPTER 6: THE BUILDINGS WE USE

1. The Americans with Disabilities Act (1990) was established by the federal government to help ensure that those with disabilities can achieve access to buildings and use the building's facilities. Attention to entrances and exits, moving between floors, moving within the building and each room, and use of water fountains, restroom facilities, and seating and tables is necessary. From a faith perspective, fulfilling the expectations of the ADA is an act of hospitality, seeking to invite and welcome people with limitations into our congregations.
2. For example, see: Ari Meisel, *LEED Materials: A Resource Guide to Green Building* (New York: Princeton Architectural Press, 2010), or Traci Rose Rider, Stacy Glass, and Jessica McNaughton *Understanding Green Building Materials* (New York: W. W. Norton, 2011).
3. "Water Resources," UN-Water website, www.unwater.org/statistics_res.html.
4. "Water Use," UN-Water website, www.unwater.org/statistics_use.html.
5. Ibid.
6. A helpful guide for estimating the volume of water used daily in an average home can be found in "Daily Water Use at Home" at www.swfwmd.state.fl.us/publications/files/daily_water_use.pdf.
7. Historically, churches have been oriented along an east-west axis, with the altar toward the east wall of the worship space, to associate the encounter with Christ in the Eucharistic celebration with the rising sun. The theological rationale for this orientation is complemented by the environmental advantages of an east-west axis. A similar correlation between theological significance and environmental stewardship can be discerned in synagogue design in North America when the ark is retained as a central liturgical focal point of the space for worship and located on the east wall, the direction of Jerusalem.
8. "Low-Emissivity Window Glazing or Glass," US Department of Energy website, www.energysavers.gov/your_home/windows_doors_skylights/index.cfm/mytopic=13430.

9. Additional information about the Green Power Network can be found at the US Department of Energy website, "About the Green Power Network," http://apps3.eere.energy.gov/ greenpower/about/index.shtml. Information concerning green power markets, green power providers, buying green power, consumer protection, and publications about green power can be found here.

10. Hall's glass work and writings are featured via her Sarah Hall Studio website, www.sarahhallstudio.com.

11. Books featuring Hall's work include J. S. Porter, *The Glass Art of Sarah Hall* (Paderborn, Germany: Glasmalerei Peters Gmbh, 2011); Sarah Hall, *The Color of Light* (Chicago: Liturgy Training Publications, 1999); and Bob Shantz and Sarah Hall, *Windows on Our Souls* (Toronto: Novalis, 2007).

12. Information about small wind energy systems can be found at the US Department of Energy's website: http://www1.eere. energy.gov/wind/ and http://www.energysavers.gov/renewable_ energy/wind/index.cfm/mytopic=50014.

13. See "geothermal heat pumps" at www.energysavers.gov.

14. Martha McDonald, "Energy Efficiency" (June 2006), at http. traditional-building.com.

15. Interview conducted on October 20, 2009.

Chapter 7: The Interior Environments in Which We Live

1. "Buildings and Their Impact on the Environment: A Statistical Summary," United States Environmental Protection Agency, revised April 22, 2009, p. 4, at www.epa.gov/greenbuilding/ pubs/gbstats.pdf

2. "An Introduction to Indoor Air Quality (IAQ)," United States Environmental Protection Agency, at www.epa.gov/iaq/voc. html

3. Tracy Rose Rider, *Understanding Green Building Guidelines for Students and Young Professionals* (New York: W. W. Norton, 2009), 51.

4. "Light Bulbs (CFLs): Did You Know?," at www.en-ergystar.gov/index.cfm?fuseaction=find_a_product. showProductGroup&pgw_code=LB.

5. Using incandescent bulbs rather than CFLs does not reduce our exposure to mercury. According to the EPA, one-half of the 103 metric tons of mercury that the United States produces in emissions each year is generated by coal-fired power plants. Because incandescent bulbs require much more energy for

use, a little more than three times more mercury is potentially released into our environment through powering them than would be generated by using CFLs. See "Frequently Asked Questions: Information on Compact Fluorescent Light Bulbs (CFLs) and Mercury, November 2010," at www.energystar.gov/ia/partners/promotions/change_light/downloads/Fact_Sheet_Mercury.pdf

6. For some recent developments in the discussion, see "Will LED Light Bulbs Best Your CFLs and Incandescents?" *Popular Mechanics*, August 4, 2010, at http.popularmechanics.com/science/environment/will-led-light-bulbs-best-cfls-and-incandescents

7. See "Energy Savers," US Department of Energy website, www.energysavers.gov/your_home/energy_audits/index.cfm/mytopic=11160.

Glossary

altar: The table in a Christian worship space on which the eucharistic elements of bread and wine are consecrated. The table may be simple or ornate and made of wood, stone, or other substantial material. The term *altar* tends to be used in traditions that are more formal in their liturgical celebrations.

ark: The cabinet or container for the Torah scrolls in a synagogue, reminiscent of the Ark of the Covenant. The ark is usually located next to a wall that faces Jerusalem (in North America, the eastern wall).

automatic fixture sensors: Motion-detecting sensors that can automatically activate lighting, faucets, toilets, urinals, and paper towel dispensers.

bimah: The platform from which a service may be led. It holds the desk from which the Torah is read in synagogue celebrations.

bioswale: A constructed vegetative area, such as a ditch or depression, designed to absorb and process contaminants in runoff storm water. The areas are composed of uncompacted substrate containing soil, sand, gravel, rock, and organic materials. Different zones within the bioswale will be planted with varying indigenous species of plants that can tolerate a range of water conditions, from standing water in the lowest elevation zone to drier conditions in the highest zone.

blackwater: Usually defined as wastewater from toilets. Blackwater contains potentially toxic material and must be subject to appropriate sewage treatment. It may not be reused directly for irrigation. Some jurisdictions may classify certain types of greywater as blackwater as well.

brownfield property: Developed land that has been used for industrial or certain commercial purposes but no longer is being used for those purposes. Often the site is environmentally contaminated, and financial incentives may be provided by city, state, or federal sources for its redevelopment.

clerestory: Windows located in an exterior wall that rises above an adjoining roof. Clerestory can provide additional natural light to centrally located interior spaces.

columbarium: A repository for vessels containing cremated remains. An interior room or outdoor space may be set aside for this purpose.

compact fluorescent lamp or light (or CFL): A lamp that uses less energy and generates less heat than a conventional incandescent lamp or bulb. Those intended to replace household incandescent lamps are constructed of thin gas-filled tubing in various patterns and an integrated ballast and are fitted with a standard screw base. Other bases are available for commercial fixtures.

constructed wetlands: A constructed marsh-type vegetative area designed to absorb and process contaminants in runoff storm water. Wetlands are intended to retain moisture over long periods of time. Indigenous species of plants that can tolerate long-term submergence are necessary for wetland areas.

curtain wall: A non-load-bearing wall or skin located between structural members. Glass, metal, or other types of materials can be used for this type of wall.

daylight harvesting: Maximizing the collection and use of natural light in a building.

daylighting: The controlled use of natural light in ways that decrease the need for artificial illumination.

detention basin (or dry ponds): A planted area intended to provide a temporary location for storm water to gather and gradually disperse. Detention basins are important for flood

control and combating soil erosion. Because they are intended
to primarily direct water, they do not provide much filtration for improving water quality (bioswales and constructed
wetlands provide more of a filtration role).

ecological footprint: A relative measure of the resources consumed and waste produced by an individual or community.

gabion wall: Metal cages filled with rubble that are assembled
into walls. Usually gabion walls are used as retaining walls,
but alternative purposes are emerging.

glazing: With respect to architecture, application of glass to openings in a building. A glazed surface is one composed of glass.

green design: Augmenting design to improve environmental impact, such as conserving energy or using renewable resources.
Green design aims to minimize the negative impact of a product or building on the environment.

green roof: A roof covering usually composed of vegetation,
engineered soil, and a waterproof membrane. This type of
roof assists with storm-water management (absorbs and
filters rainwater), insulates the building it covers (helping with
energy costs and reducing heat island effect), and enhances
general air quality (plants excrete oxygen). Also called "vegetative" or "vegetated" roofs. Green roofs can provide an oasis
of beauty in developed urban areas. A range of green roofs
can be designed.

greenfield property: Land that remains in its natural state (undeveloped) or has been used only for agricultural purposes.
Greenfield sites are generally found on the edges of urban or
suburban areas or between them.

greywater: Wastewater from sinks (household wastewater), baths,
showers, and washing machines. Greywater does contain
bacteria and other potential pathogens and must be properly
filtered. In some areas of the country greywater is reclaimed
for limited reuse.

heat island effect: Suburban and urban areas generally develop
increased levels of heat due in part to the fact that buildings
and paved areas absorb, trap, and radiate heat. The cumulative

impact of this heat cycle raises the ambient temperature of developed areas.

indigenous: In this book, plants and wildlife native to a particular locale. An example would be prairie grasses and flowers that were once widely distributed across the Midwestern United States. Contemporary agricultural development removed the original prairie plantings in favor of cultivated field and vegetable crops, and residential and commercial property development has displaced many more acres.

land grading: The movement of earth on a building site in order to develop the property for the intended uses of the community. The land may require leveling, specific slopes for drainage, roadways, or landscape features. Minimizing grading of the natural surface is an important way to preserve natural drainage, features, wildlife, plantings, and topsoil.

light pollution: Excess artificial light that negatively affects the surrounding natural environment. Outdoor lighting for parking and walking areas are a primary source of light pollution, although unnecessary levels of interior illumination that spill out of glazed surfaces (areas of glass) during evening hours can also contribute to this phenomenon.

light shelf: A horizontal overhang placed adjacent to a window. A light shelf has a highly reflective upper surface. It can be located on the interior or exterior of a building. The shelf can redirect natural light deeper into an interior space and can also provide shading.

low-E glass: Glass that has been treated with a special low-emissivity coating. The coating is either a metal or a metallic oxide layer deposited on the glass. The coating is applied to help control heat transfer. Glass treated in this way is called Low-E glass. Many windows are made with Low-E glass today, a feature that increases their insulation value (R-value). Low-E glass has been found to reduce energy loss by as much as 30 to 50 percent.

millwork: Manufactured wood products for interior environments, including doors, window casings, cabinets, paneling, baseboards, and moldings.

ner tamid: The eternal lamp or light located above the ark in a synagogue. The light is a symbol of God's eternal and imminent presence. The *ner tamid* is to be perpetually lit, and is a good candidate for powering with photovoltaic cells.

open space: Land left intentionally undeveloped in an effort to preserve the natural resources and beauty of a particular site.

R-value: R-value measures the resistance (hence, *R*) ability of a product to impede heat flow through it. The higher the R-value of the product the more effective the insulating property it possesses. Different climatic conditions will suggest different R-values as necessary for buildings.

radiant barrier: A physical material intended to reduce the level of heat absorbed by a surface. Highly reflective materials are used as radiant barriers.

radiant heat: Heat transmitted through direct exposure to a source, such as the sun.

restorative design: Includes an effort to incorporate sustainable design, but makes a commitment to achieving an ultimate design that will yield a higher level of natural health than was originally measured in relation to a particular site. Restorative design seeks to enhance the quality of land, water, and air rather than stop at having a minimal or zero impact.

retention basin (or wet ponds): A planted area intended to provide a location for storm water to gather and remain for an extended period of time. In addition to providing flood protection and combating soil erosion, retention basins aid in recharging groundwater sources and can provide a level of water filtration. Bioswales and constructed wetlands are more developed expressions of a retention basin.

simcha: Derived from the Hebrew word for joy, it can refer to a happy or festive occasion, such as a wedding or religious rite of passage.

smart growth: A design approach to developing urban and suburban communities that values a sustainable balance between undeveloped and developed land. After careful study, limits on the growth boundary of a community will be established to encourage more compact development and preservation of natural environments.

sprawl: Unrestricted, ever-expanding growth and development of urban and suburban areas. Sprawl is fueled by economic, social, and political forces and yields, perhaps unintentionally, negative consequences, such as the rapid destruction of natural habitats, increased distancing of people within developed areas (physically and psychologically), and increased dependency on vehicular transportation and infrastructure, including increasing paved areas for roads and parking, resources for fuel, and emissions from fuel production and vehicle use.

storm-water runoff: The rainwater that gathers and runs over conventional roads, parking areas, paved walkways, and roofs. The usually impervious nature of these manmade surfaces creates large quantities of water that will need to be directed to appropriate areas for absorption into the earth.

sustainable design: Includes an effort to incorporate green design, but makes a commitment to achieving an ultimate design that will yield a zero or near zero impact on the environment. Sustainable design seeks to consume no more energy than it generates, uses only renewable materials at an appropriate rate, and excretes no waste beyond that which can be absorbed and processed by the natural environment.

Torah ark: See "ark."

Trombe wall: A thick south-facing wall (in the Northern Hemisphere), often coated black and made of a material intended to absorb energy from the sun. A clear glazing panel is attached a few inches away from the surface of the wall to assist with heat retention. Vents are located in the top and bottom portions of the wall. Heat gradually builds up in the wall during the day and is released into the building at night via the wall itself and the vents. A natural air current is established, with warm air rising and entering the building through the upper vent and cool air moving from the inside toward the exterior glazing through the lower vent. Overhang placement and adding exterior vents can adjust heat generation and direction in summer months.

vegetative roof: See "green roof."

vernacular design: Architectural design inspired by unpretentious, often simple design as found in agricultural buildings such as barns or silos, residential houses, and industrial structures such as factories or foundries.

Selected and Annotated Bibliography

BIBLICAL AND THEOLOGICAL RESOURCES

Bergant, Dianne. *The Earth Is the Lord's: The Bible, Ecology, and Worship*. American Essays in Liturgy. Collegeville, MN: Liturgical Press, 1998. A Christian examination of both testaments of Scripture from the perspective that the earth is God's creation and humanity has been given responsibilities to care for it.

Bernstein, Ellen, ed. *Ecology and the Jewish Spirit: Where Nature and the Sacred Meet*. Woodstock, VT: Jewish Lights Publishing, 1998. Thirty-seven essays organized according to ecological reflections in relation to the sacrality of place, time, and community.

———. *The Splendor of Creation: A Biblical Ecology*. Cleveland: Pilgrim Press, 2005. Founder and long-time director of Shomrei Adamah, Keepers of the Earth, Bernstein articulates a poetic and substantial ecological reading of Genesis 1 and the seven days of creation.

Bernstein, Ellen, and David Fink. *Let the Earth Teach You Torah*. Philadelphia: Shomrei Adamah, 1992. A practical guidebook intended to assist congregations in understanding Jewish perspectives on the relationship between humanity and nature. Includes many readings and interactive exercises.

Bouma-Prediger, Steven. *For the Beauty of the Earth: A Christian Vision for Creation Care.* 2nd ed. Grand Rapids: Baker Academic, 2010. A substantial evangelical response calling for active Christian engagement in environmental care as a faith mandate.

Brown, Edward. *Our Father's World: Mobilizing the Church to Care for the Creation.* South Hadley, MA: Doorlight Publications, 2006. A publication from Care of Creation, a Christian environmental organization that seeks to resource faith communities for creation care. Chapter 9 explicitly mentions addressing creation care through responsible use of the land and buildings owned by churches, including use of the LEED program.

Conradie, Ernst M. *An Ecological Christian Anthropology: At Home on Earth?* Aldershot, UK: Ashgate Publishing, 2005. Conradie pursues a theological approach that accents the role humanity has been given to contribute to the redemption of creation versus redemption from creation.

Edwards, Denis. *Ecology at the Heart of Faith.* Maryknoll, NY: Orbis Books, 2006. Written particularly from a Roman Catholic perspective, this book explores biblical, theological, and sacramental dimensions of creation care. Special attention is made to root a holistic understanding of earth stewardship in the fullness of the Trinity.

Elon, Ari, Naomi Mara Hyman, and Arthur Waskow, eds. *Trees, Earth and Torah: A Tu B'Shvat Anthology.* Philadelphia: Jewish Publication Society, 1999. A collection of substantial reflections concerning the festival of *Tu B'Shvat* from the perspectives of biblical and rabbinic Judaism, Kabbalah and Hasidism, Zionism, and eco-Judaism.

Foltz, Richard C., ed. *Worldviews, Religion, and the Environment: A Global Anthology.* Belmont, CA: Thomson Learning/ Wadsworth, 2003. Essays pertaining to Judaism by A. Hütterman, T. Frymer-Kensky, S. Schwarzschild, and A. Waskow are included in this collection. Essays pertaining to Christianity by A. Peterson, S. McFague, J. Chryssavgis, C. Dewitt, and T. Berry are included as well.

Gottlieb, Roger S., ed. *This Sacred Earth: Religion, Nature, Environment.* 2nd ed. New York: Routledge, 2004. Essays pertaining to Judaism by D. Swartz, A. Waskow, I. Diamond and D. Seidenberg, E. Bernstein and D. Fink, and S. Zuckerman are included in this collection. Essays pertaining to Christianity by A. Peterson, Pope John Paul II, Ecumenical Patriarch Bartholomew, J. Haught, J. Cobb, S. McFague, T. Walker, R. Ruether, I. Gebara, T. Berry, and S. Taylor are included in this collection. Multiple Christian denominational statements are also reproduced in this collection of essays.

Hessel, Dieter T., and Rosemary Radford Ruether, eds. *Christianity and Ecology: Seeking the Well-Being of Earth and Humans.* Cambridge, MA: Harvard University Press, 2000. A collection of more than twenty-five essays exploring a range of theological responses to environmental care. Contributors in addition to the editors include Elizabeth A. Johnson, Sallie McFague, John Chryssavgis, Thomas Berry, Catherine Keller, James A. Nash, Calvin DeWitt, Ian G. Barbour, John B. Cobb Jr., and Larry Rasmussen.

Hillel, Daniel. *The Natural History of the Bible: An Environmental Exploration of the Hebrew Scriptures.* New York: Columbia University Press, 2006. A systematic analysis of discrete periods of Israelite history in their historical contexts, focusing on the development of the Hebrew Scriptures in relation to the natural environment.

Lodge, David M., and Christopher Hamlin, eds. *Religion and the New Ecology: Environmental Responsibility in a World of Flux.* Notre Dame: University of Notre Dame Press, 2006. A series of essays considering Judeo-Christian responses to environmental issues from historical, theological, and ethical perspectives. In addition to the editors, Elspeth Whitney, Eugene Cittadino, Gary E. Belovsky, Patricia Ann Fleming, John F. Haught, and Larry Rasmussen have contributed work to this collection.

Oelschlaeger, Max. *Caring for Creation: An Ecumenical Approach to the Environmental Crisis.* New Haven, CT: Yale University Press, 1994. Oelschlaeger looks at the spectrum of responses

to ecological issues within both Jewish and Christian traditions. This study emphasizes taking religion seriously as a
force for social good in relation to the environment.

Van Dyke, Fred, David C. Mahan, Joseph K. Sheldon, and Ray-
mond H. Brand. *Redeeming Creation: The Biblical Basis for
Environmental Stewardship.* Downers Grove, IL: InterVarsity
Press, 1996. A Christian systematic study of biblical understandings that seeks to substantiate a mandate for creation
care. Chapter 9 mentions church design as a way to contribute
to ecological stewardship.

Waskow, Arthur, ed. *Torah of the Earth: Exploring 4,000 Years
of Ecology in Jewish Thought.* 2 vols. Woodstock, VT: Jewish
Lights Publishing, 2000. Volume 1 includes essays categorized
under the headings "Biblical Israel" and "Rabbinic Judaism."
Volume 2 includes essays categorized under the headings
"Zionism" and "Eco-Judaism."

CONGREGATIONAL ARTICLES AND RESOURCES

Cannon, Patrick F., and James Caulfield. *Frank Lloyd Wright's
Unity Temple: A Good Time Place.* Petaluma, CA: Pomegran-
ate Communications, 2009. A brief historical exploration of
Frank Lloyd Wright and his work on Unity Temple, Oak Park,
Illinois.

Chiotti, Roberto. "The Architecture of Eco-Theology." *Faith and
Form* 41, no. 1 (2008): 6–11. Features the theological under-
standings that guided the green design of St. Gabriel of the
Sorrowful Virgin, Toronto.

———. "Colouring Your New Church Green." *Celebrate!* 45, no.
5 (September–October 2006): 4–7. Features the green design
of St. Gabriel of the Sorrowful Virgin, Toronto.

———. "LEEDing the Way: The New St. Gabriel's Church."
Celebrate! 45, no. 6 (November–December 2006): 3–6. Fea-
tures the green design of St. Gabriel of the Sorrowful Virgin,
Toronto.

Chiotti, Roberto, and Richard S. Vosko. "Worship Space Today." *America* 204, no. 17 (May 23, 2011): 14–16. Features St. Gabriel of the Sorrowful Virgin, Toronto, and its green approach to design.

Crosbie, Michael J. "Green Synagogue." *Architecture Week,* no. 423 (April 15, 2009), www.architectureweek.com. Features the LEED platinum-rated dimensions of Jewish Reconstructionist Congregation, Evanston, Illinois.

Grant, Al, and De Herman, eds. *Green Shalom Action Guide.* Kensington, MD: Temple Emanuel, 2006. The guide includes details concerning Temple Emanuel's journey in pursuit of sustainable living, current policies, and strategies for fulfilling their ongoing commitment to environmental stewardship.

Lechner, Sheryl. "A DC Temple's Quest to Live Lightly on the Earth." *Reform Judaism* (Summer 2005): 41–42, 44–45. Features the creation care activities of Temple Emanuel, Kensington, Maryland.

Malin, Nadav. "Congregation Takes Charge." *GreenSource* 5, no. 6 (2010): 101. Features the sustainable design achieved by Jewish Reconstructionist Congregation, Evanston, Illinois.

Moline, Ron. *In Good Faith: Compiled from the Archives of the Unity Temple Unitarian Universalist Congregation of Oak Park.* Bloomington, IN: Xlibris, 2008. Archival materials from Unity Temple, Oak Park, are gleaned to provide insight into the congregation's development.

Ontario Cast-In-Place Concrete Development Council, "St. Gabriel's Passionist Church," *Case Study* 5, no. 1 (n.d.). Features the green design of St. Gabriel of the Sorrowful Virgin, Toronto.

Polland, Annie. *Landmark of the Spirit: The Eldridge Street Synagogue.* New Haven, CT: Yale University Press, 2009. A historical exploration of the people and achievements of Eldridge Street Synagogue, New York.

Siry, Joseph M. *Unity Temple: Frank Lloyd Wright and Architecture for Liberal Religion.* Cambridge, UK: Cambridge University Press, 1998. A historical exploration of Frank Lloyd Wright and his work on Unity Temple, Oak Park, Illinois.

Thompson, Livia D. "Where You LEED, I Will Follow." *NATA Journal* 43, no. 2 (Fall 2008/5769): 6–9. This issue of the National Association of Temple Administrators is devoted to creation care. Entitled "The Greening Issue," the Thompson article features Congregation Beth David, San Luis Obispo, California, and Jewish Reconstructionist Congregation, Evanston, Illinois. Multiple other articles provide strategies and resources for pursuing environmentally sustainable congregational life.

Union for Reform Judaism. *Rejoice in Your Handiwork: Sacred Space and Synagogue Architecture*. 2 parts. New York: Union for Reform Judaism, 2005. Congregation Beth David, San Luis Obispo, California, is featured in part 2 of this publication.

Walker, Alissa. "Green, Pray, Love: A New Synagogue Wins LEED's Highest Accolade." *I.D.* 56, no. 2 (March–April 2009): 24–25. Features Jewish Reconstruction Congregation, Evanston, Illinois.

Yearwood, Pauline Dubkin. "Constructing Values." *Chicago's Green Synagogue. The Chicago Jewish News*. Special Issue (n.d.): 3–4. Features Jewish Reconstruction Congregation, Evanston, Illinois.

———. "Green in the Details." *Chicago's Green Synagogue. The Chicago Jewish News*. Special Issue (n.d.): 7–10. Features Jewish Reconstruction Congregation, Evanston, Illinois.

ECUMENICAL AND DENOMINATIONAL RESOURCES

District of Columbia Energy Office. *The Green Faith Guide: Working Together to Protect and Restore Our Environment*. Washington, DC: District of Columbia Energy Office, 2004. An interfaith guide for sharing sustainable ideas related to congregational life, including short chapters on green building, and which seeks to foster cooperation between faith traditions.

Faith and the Common Good. *Greening Sacred Spaces Health and Sustainability Guide: Greening Daily Operation[s] for Faith Communities.* Cambridge, ON: Faith and the Common Good. No date. Available on-line as a PDF document at: http://www.greeningsacredspaces.net/files/GSS%20Health%20and%20Sustainability%20Guide-Greening%20Daily%20Operation%20for%20Faith%20Communities.pdf. An 88-page guide from Faith and the Common Good, an interfaith network of people based in the Toronto area. The guide provides information to congregations on local and regional products for green building and cleaning.

Hall, Sarah. *The Color of Light: Commissioning Stained Glass for a Church.* Chicago: Liturgy Training Publications, 1999. A helpful congregational handbook for understanding basic principles behind the creation, commissioning, and preserving of glass installations.

National Council of Churches, USA. *Building a Firm Foundation: A Creation-Friendly Building Guide for Churches.* New York: National Council of Churches, USA/Eco-Justice Program, 2006.

Porter, J. S. *The Glass Art of Sarah Hall.* Paderborn, Germany: Glasmalerei Peters Gmbh, 2011. Features glass by artist Sarah Hall, including installations that incorporate solar cells into the design.

Union for Reform Judaism. *Rejoice in Your Handiwork: Sacred Space and Synagogue Architecture.* 2 parts. New York: Union for Reform Judaism, 2005. Part one is subtitled "Congregational Guide to the Process of Renovating and Building." Part two is subtitled "Form and Function: Design Considerations for Congregations."

Unitarian Universalist Association of Congregations. *Green Sanctuary Manual.* 5th ed. Boston: Unitarian Universalist Association of Congregations, 2009.

United Jewish Appeal-Federation of New York. *The Greening Guide: UJA-Federation of New York Network Greening Initiative.* New York: UJA-Federation of New York, 2008.

United States Conference of Catholic Bishops. *Renewing the Earth: An Invitation to Reflection and Action on Environment in Light of Catholic Social Teaching.* Washington, DC: United States Conference of Catholic Bishops, 1991.

Nonreligious Green Building Resources

American Society of Heating, Refrigerating and Air-Conditioning Engineers. *ASHRAE Green Guide: The Design, Construction, and Operation of Sustainable Buildings.* 3rd ed. Burlington, MA: Butterworth-Heinemann/Elsevier, 2010. A technical resource to guide the work of professionals. Provides excellent guidance for incorporating green strategies in relation to HVAC, electrical, and plumbing designs for new construction and existing buildings, including the pros and cons of various options.

Jones, Louise, ed. *Environmentally Responsible Design: Green and Sustainable Design for Interior Designers.* Hoboken, NJ: John Wiley and Sons, 2008. A series of articles addressing various dimensions of interior design, including air quality, HVAC systems, finishes, and furnishings. Part 4 is of special interest in that it features a case study of the sustainable design efforts of the Immaculate Heart of Mary Motherhouse, Monroe, Michigan.

Meisel, Ari. *LEED Materials: A Resource Guide to Green Building.* New York: Princeton Architectural Press, 2010. A comprehensive guide to products and materials that will gain LEED credits, from site development to final finishes and furnishings.

Mendler, Sandra, William Odell, and Mary Ann Lazarus. *The HOK Guidebook to Sustainable Design.* 2nd ed. Hoboken, NJ: John Wiley and Sons, 2006. Architects from Hellmuth, Obata, and Kassabaum have collaborated on this resource for architects, engineers, and designers as a primer to achieving sustainable structures and environments. The importance of integration and process are emphasized. The second edition is written to complement the LEED criteria for measuring environmental design.

Montoya, Michael. *Green Building Fundamentals: A Practical Guide to Understanding and Applying Fundamental Sustainable Construction Practices and the LEED Green Building Rating System.* 2nd ed. Upper Saddle River, NJ: Prentice-Hall, 2011. Montoya has provided a user-friendly overview of sustainable design and green building in light of the LEED, version 3.0, criteria. Chapters address dimensions of sustainable sites, water efficiency, energy efficiency and alternative sources, indoor environmental quality, and materials for preparing to be a certified LEED professional.

Reeder, Linda. *Guide to Green Building Rating Systems: Understanding LEED, Green Globes, ENERGY STAR, the National Green Building Standard (NAHB), and More.* Hoboken, NJ: John Wiley and Sons, 2010. A useful guide for comparing and contrasting prominent national green building rating systems. Also included are chapters addressing local and international programs.

Rider, Traci Rose. *Understanding Green Building Guidelines for Students and Young Professionals.* Edited by Karen Levine. New York: W. W. Norton, 2009. A brief and helpful guide for comparing four primary systems for green building: Leadership in Energy and Environmental Design (LEED), the Natural Step, Green Globes, and the National Association of Home Builders (NAHB) National Green Building Program. The last chapter provides an overview of local green building guidelines produced by select United States cities.

Rider, Traci Rose, Stacy Glass, and Jessica McNaughton. *Understanding Green Building Materials.* New York: W. W. Norton, 2011. A brief and helpful guide for comprehending the range of materials available for green building. Sections addressing rating systems, certification programs, and life-cycle assessment are also included.

7Group and Bill Reed. *The Integrative Design Guide to Green Building: Redefining the Practice of Sustainability.* Hoboken,

NJ: John Wiley and Sons, 2009. Written primarily for building professionals and those interested in understanding the
theory and application of sustainable design, this book will
help the reader comprehend the range of green approaches
available today and navigate present limitations and potential.

United States Green Building Council. *Green Building Design and
Construction*. Washington, DC: US Green Building Council,
2009. The official LEED reference guide for new commercial construction and renovation. The LEED guides are most
helpful to building professionals and others pursuing LEED
certification projects. In addition to details concerning LEED
certification and documents, a twenty-page glossary explains
technical terms related to sustainable building.

———. *Green Interior Design and Construction*. Washington,
DC: US Green Building Council, 2009. The official LEED
reference guide for new commercial interior construction and
renovation. The LEED guides are most helpful to building
professionals and others pursuing LEED certification projects.

———. *Green Building Operations and Maintenance*. Washington, DC: US Green Building Council, 2009. The official LEED
reference guide for commercial green building operations and
maintenance.

Winchip, Susan M. *Sustainable Design for Interior Environments*.
2nd ed. New York: Fairchild Publications, 2011. Written for
an audience ranging from students to design professionals,
this new edition contains detailed information for greening
all dimensions of interior environments and includes references to historic preservation.

Young, Robert A. *Historic Preservation Technology*. Hoboken, NJ:
John Wiley and Sons, 2008. A helpful primer addressing all
dimensions of building for historic preservation, including a
chapter devoted to sustainability.

Yudelson, Jerry. *Greening Existing Buildings*. New York: McGraw
Hill, 2010. A useful volume for exploring market implications,
rating systems, costing issues, options, best practices, and case
studies for green building.

Index